GREATEST EVER BOXING CHAMPIONS

GREATEST EVER BOXING CHAMPIONS

Their minds, their workouts and their journeys

Gary Todd

First published in 2025 by New Holland Publishers
newhollandpublishers.com

A record of this book is held at the National Library of Australia.

ISBN 9781742577104

Managing Director: Fiona Schultz
General Manager/Publisher: Olga Dementiev
Editor: Xavier Waterkeyn
Designer: Andrew Davies
Production Director: Arlene Gippert

Keep up with New Holland Publishers:
NewHollandPublishers
@newhollandpublishers

DEDICATION

To the boxers in the book. Thank you for your time, your stories and for giving me the inspiration to write. It was a labour of love, and a struggle in many ways, but it was also a pleasure and a privilege to talk and spend time with each of them.

To the men and women in the gyms around the world, who are there in the shadows, working, mentoring, caring and being there for the kids. They open the doors of the gym every day, so the kids have a safe place to go, making them feel like they are part of something special.

For the kids of today and tomorrow. Be strong inside and be kind in life. Never doubt yourself and never allow anyone to doubt you. Say no to bullies.

Love yourself and be yourself.

Always remember, things get better if you keep going strong inside.

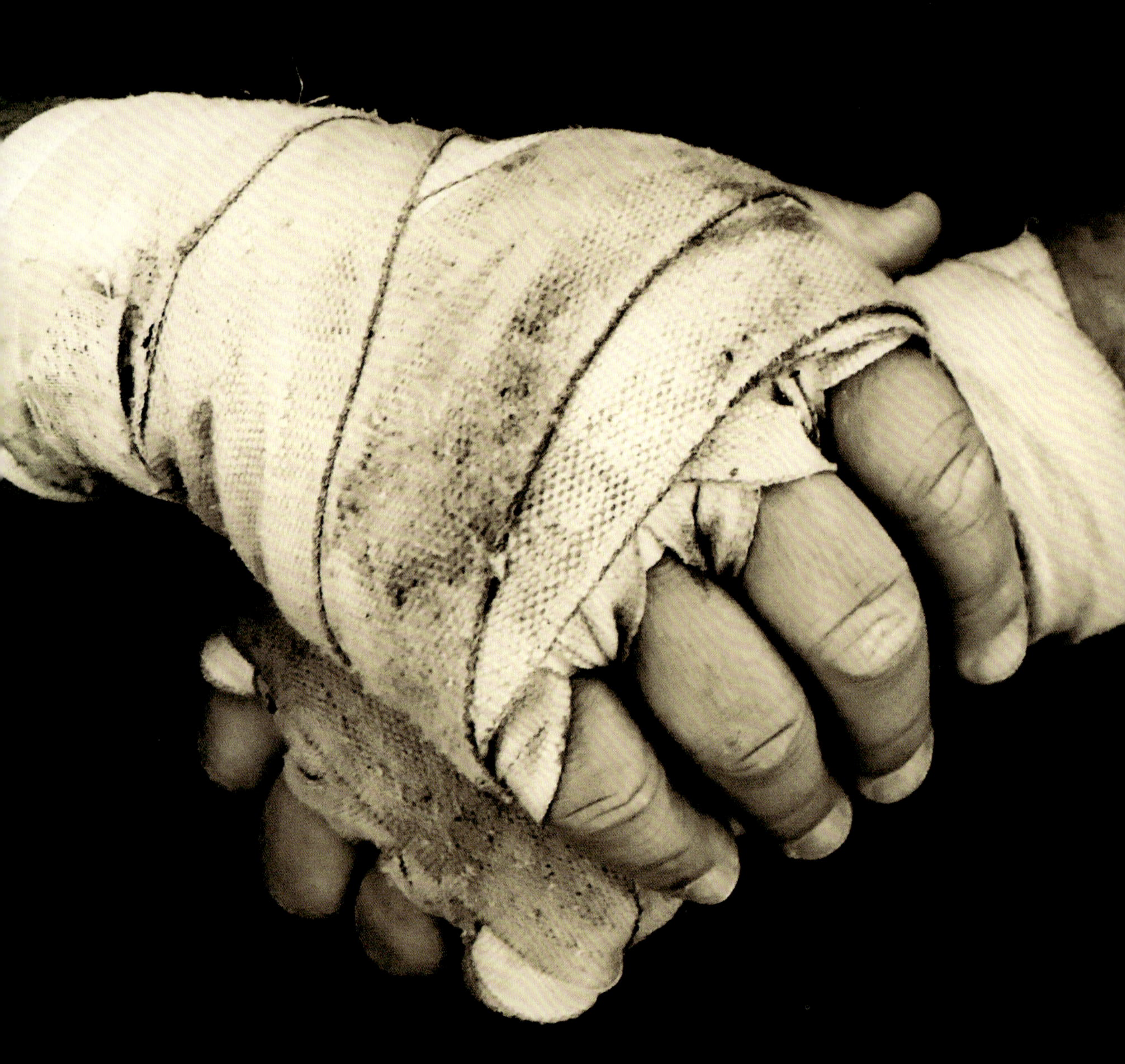

THE CHAMPION BOXERS FEATURED

FIGHTING TALK

I have always been fascinated by fighters and what they did to achieve their dreams. As a young boy in Dundee, Scotland, I would watch them on the TV. I loved watching the montage of the boxers training in the gym, punching the bags, skipping and watching their highlights in the ring. I loved their stories. Muhammad Ali, Joe Frazier, Ken Norton, Chuck Wepner, Ken Buchanan, Gerry Cooney, Jim Watt, Eusebio Pedroza, John H Stracey, John Conteh, Dave Boy Green, Tony Sibson, Azumah Nelson, Barry McGuigan, Frank Bruno, John Mugabi, Vito Antuofermo, Marvin Hagler, Thomas Hearns and Mike Tyson – just to name a few of many.

I never really had any role models when I was growing up. I had my Uncle Joe, who had been a boxer, and I had a few characters from the TV but that was it. Rocky running up the stairs in Philadelphia would always be in my mind as I would run in the snow, the wind, and the rain. They were my heroes.

Looking back, I would never have dreamed that I could ever meet them, to be talking with them and training alongside them in the gym.

I was captivated by their stories and the sacrifices they made as a boxer, and how they kept fighting through the broken promises, the injuries, the missed opportunities along the way.

Their courage in brutal fights that they won and lost, and their resilience and self-belief they each had, to keep going on the long road to glory.

To be in a sport where you have to be at your best, where there is nowhere to hide, and you have to have the mindset that you need to destroy your opponent's dreams so you can live yours. Physical, mental, and emotional attributes make us all human.

Boxers have an undeniable belief in themselves because without it, it's game over. This mindset, along with their Athleticism, movement, reflexes, speed, strength, stamina, and skill, controlled aggression and a huge heart makes them superhuman.

In these pages I have featured fighters from all around the world and to tell each of their stories. There are boxers from eras that are long gone in time and boxers that are still fighting. Heart and soul, blood and guts fighters. There are 15-round fighters and 12-round contenders – world champions and Hall of Fame legends and they all deserve to be remembered.

Every boxer has their own story and each trains differently, but they have all battled with themselves every day, while getting ready to fight. Training hard and eating little and drinking even less to make the weight so they can fight and get paid.

I hope you enjoy reading *Greatest Ever Boxing Champions*, reading their stories and learning their training secrets and my hope is that they inspire you as they have inspired me all my life.

We can't all be a Champion of the World, but we can all be the best version of ourselves every day and reach for the stars and make our own dreams and goals become a reality.

CHOCOLATE
CHAVEZ
PRO

THE BOXERS

DONT WATCH THE CLOCK
EVERLAST
SPEAK IT.

QudosBank Arena

BOXING

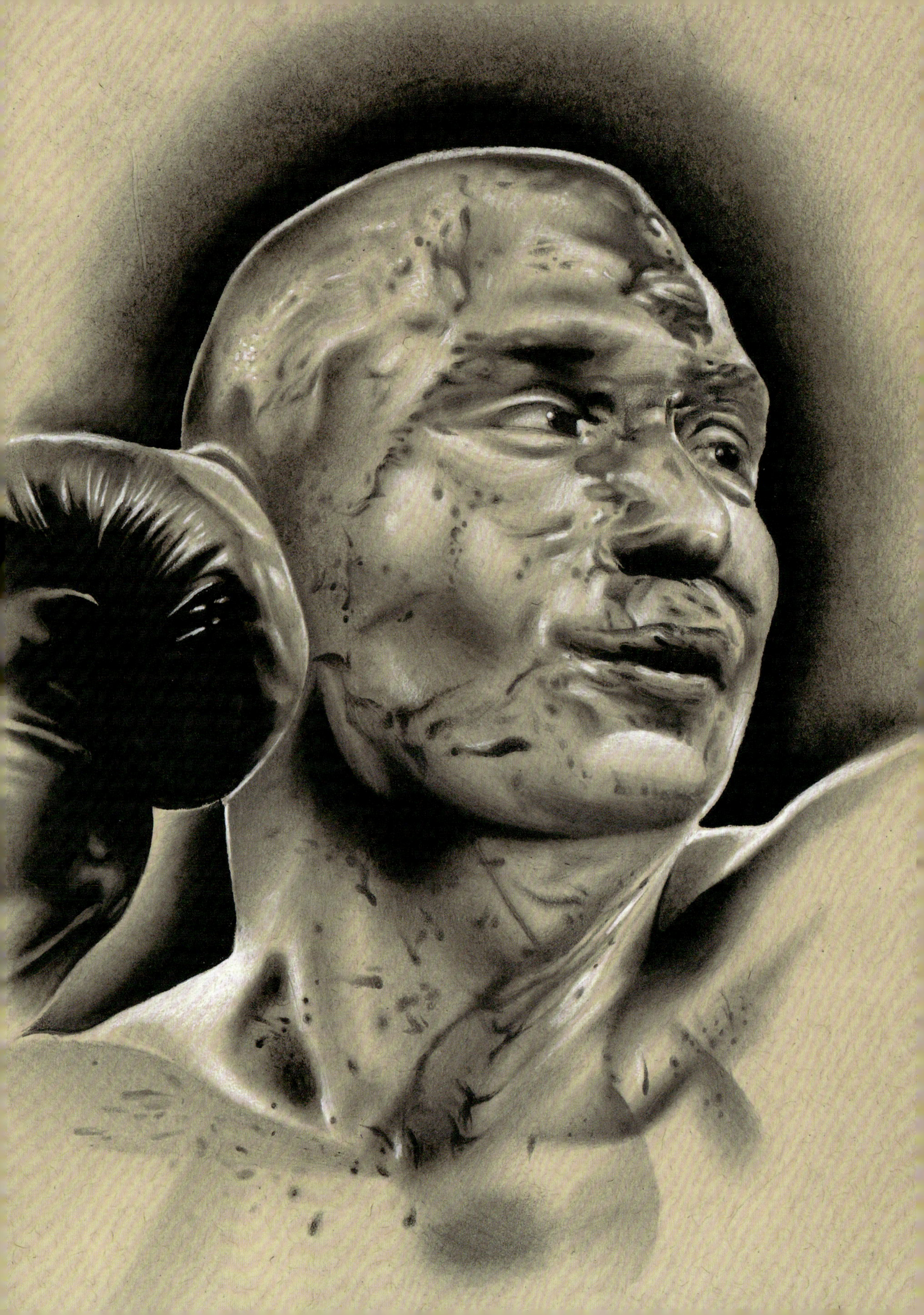

TIM TSZYU

'The Smiling Assassin'

BIOGRAPHY

In the sport of boxing, sometimes all you need is the chance to show that you belong. To do that, you need to go out and prove yourself by not just winning, not just tapping on the door of opportunity, but by breaking it down and taking it off its hinges.

Tim Tszyu (as at mid-2025 – 24 fights, 24 wins, 0 losses, 0 draws, 17 KOs) was born in 1994 and as a young boy, he was captured in his father's boxing success as a super lightweight world champion and at the age of seven, he was running around the gym with Tszyu's sparring partners, Golden Johnson, David Sample, and Gairy St Clair, watching, while his old man prepared for his world championship fights against Julio Cesar Chavez, Sharmba Mitchell, Oktay Urkal, and Zab Judah.

As a boy, he enjoyed training and being fit and strong. He enjoyed going to the beach and took to gymnastics and soccer before trying his hand at boxing. Tszyu started his amateur campaign at 15 years of age fighting a record to then turn professional in December 2016 at age 22.

The pressure on him was immense, with the media watching his every move, all the while comparing him to his hall of fame father. He just smiled.

In 2020, after beating foe after foe, he challenged fellow Australian, and former WBO welterweight world champion, Jeff Horn proving to be too much for him, with his corner stopping their fighter from further damage for an 8th round victory. Again Tszyu smiled.

With confidence growing fight by fight, he was setting his opponents up and it seemed he was knocking them down just for the fun of it.

In 2021, Tszyu faced the Japanese brawler, Takeshi Inoue.

The Japanese strongman had challenged the tough Mexican world champion, Jaime Munguia, for his WBO Super Welterweight title and took him the distance, losing on points so Tszyu would have to be at his best to withstand the challenge. In the fight, Tszyu threw every punch he could summon and although he battered Inoue, the proud, stubborn warrior wouldn't take a backward step nor would he fall, going the championship distance. With 20 fights behind him, all the talk was fighting for a world title and fighting the best at 154 pounds – 69.85 kilos.

Next up for Tszyu was the Olympian, Terrell Gausha, and this was to be Tszyu's introduction to an American audience, so he had to make a strong statement.

Gausha was a boxer, not a devastating puncher and he had experience at the top level sharing the ring with champions, Erislandy Lara, Austin Trout, and Erickson Lubin, so all eyes were again on Tszyu to see what he could do. In the fight, the thirty-three-year-old Gausha summoned every bit of his strength by knocking down the Australian in the first round and then the stamina and resilience to withstand the pressure and attack to take Tszyu the distance in Minneapolis. With this win, the door had opened slightly but not enough. There was more talk of fighting the big names and fighting for a world title, but it seemed the door was closed, for now.

Tszyu smiled again and next up was the former WBC junior middleweight world champion, Tony Harrison. The Detroit fighter had beaten Jermell Charlo on points in 2018 and had shared the ring with good fighters in his career and after losing his world title to Charlo in the rematch, this was his last chance at the championship level. Tszyu never gave him a chance, hammering him into a shock like trance, and knocking him out in the 9th round, winning the WBO interim junior middleweight title in Sydney. Three months later, he made his first defence of his newly won title, obliterating the Mexican, Carlos Ocampo in 77 seconds.

Tszyu was elevated to champion of the world status by the WBO, and this news was timely as his next opponent was the experienced and hard punching fighter, Brian Mendoza.

The man known as 'La Bala' which translated to 'the bullet' was gunning for Tszyu and he wasn't coming to Australia to see kangaroos. Mendoza had relieved the six-foot power punching interim champion, Sebastian Fundora, of his title and his senses a few months earlier and it was clear he was coming to win down under.

Tszyu left no stone unturned and trained intensely for the American puncher and in the fight, Tszyu was visibly stronger and sharper, hurting Mendoza and leaving him panting for air, and holding on and surviving the full twelve rounds. Harrison and Ocampo have not fought since. Mendoza was beaten in his last fight, losing to Serhii Bohachuk in March 2024.

Tszyu was a sensation in Australia. A promoters dream and he was a world champion in the prime of his life. He had made a lot of money and life was good, but for some, it's just not enough. Tszyu wants more. He was hungry for success. He wanted to be the undisputed champion at 154 pounds – 69 kilos.

As I took my first step to the stairs of the Tszyu gym, memories of twenty years ago flooded back. As I climbed the stairs, I had Kostya Tszyu in my mind's eye, until I pushed open the door to the gym and I saw Tim Tszyu standing there smiling, as he wrapped his hands. In my mind's eye, I could see him as a young boy running around the gym with his dad staring at a spot on the wall, while skipping to a beat only he could hear. It was a surreal moment.

After the Mendoza fight, Tszyu announced that he would be making a full-on assault in America, fighting any of the top fighters and there were some pretty big hitters on his list.

To the surprise of many, it was then announced that Keith Thurman was up next. Thurman was moving up in weight to challenge Tszyu at a contracted catch weight of 155 lbs – 70 kilos.

The obvious questions is why would he come back at all after yet another long layoff?

At age 35, with a long career and injuries a plenty, and a stack of good paydays, why would he come back again? The only thing that was driving Thurman was his self-belief, his ego, and the chance to dethrone the younger Tszyu.

After a lot of smack talk by Thurman, it was reported that he had injured himself in training, rupturing his bicep, forcing him to pull out of the fight. With only eleven days to go, and the fight in jeopardy, Tszyu's people had to find an opponent of note to step in. After a few days, it was announced that Tszyu would be facing Sebastian Fundora for the WBO and the WBC Junior middleweight titles.

Fundora (23 wins, 1 loss 1 draw) was known as 'The Towering Inferno' and at 6'6, with long arms, he boxed as a southpaw since he was a nine-year-old boy in Tampa, Florida. He came from a proud boxing family of Mexican and Cuban heritage. He turned professional in 2016. After racking up thirteen victories by stopping his opponents, he fought Brian Mendoza in 2023, and in a fight he was winning on points, he was knocked out by a tremendous combination from Mendoza in the seventh round, which sent him crumbling to the canvas. Fundora was originally slotted in to return to the ring, to face the 6'0 Ukrainian knockout artist, Serhii Bohachuk for the interim WBC junior middleweight title on the undercard.

Tszyu's former opponent, Brian Mendoza stepped in to fight Bohachuk, and the Tszyu v Fundora unification fight was on.

In the fight, the size and reach difference was obvious, but Tszyu was pressing and pressuring Fundora while looking to get inside and land his right hand. Tszyu was looking solid, coming forward aggressively until an exchange inside, and an accidental elbow from Fundora, opened a deep gash to the top of Tszyu's hair line in the second round. With blood pouring down his face, and into his eyes, Tszyu kept fighting.

The ringside doctor had a look at the cut and allowed the fight to continue. Many wouldn't have.

Tszyu's face was a mask of blood, and as he pushed Fundora back, getting inside, he was landing with hard punches that was causing damage, busting and breaking Fundora's nose.

With blood splattered all over the two warriors, they both bit down hard on their gum shields, each man fighting with pride and courage in a bloody war that went the championship distance. After twelve rounds, Fundora had done enough, using his long solid jab to pepper Tszyu, and win by a split decision to become the unified champion of the world in 2024. Fundora would also make history along with his sister, Gabriela, as the only sister and brother to be world champions at the same time.

Tszyu returned to Australia to rest and heal, and it was announced that he would be facing the hard punching Texan, Vergil Ortiz in Los Angeles in the August of 2024.

The 5'10, Ortiz (21 wins, 0 losses with 20 KOs) was a force at welterweight but at 26, he struggled to make the championship weight of 147 pounds – 66.6 kilos – so it was time to move up. In April 2024, Ortiz, fighting at junior middleweight, destroyed Thomas Dulorme in the first round with a vicious well placed left hook shot to the liver to stake his claim to challenge the twenty-nine-year-old Tszyu.

In the lead up to the fight, Tszyu travelled to the heat and humidity in the jungles of Thailand where he met his father where they trained together, working on tactics and old school grind to get ready for Ortiz.

With nine weeks to go, it was announced that Tszyu v Ortiz was off due to the Australian fighter's doctor advising him to give the cut more time to heal properly. For Tszyu, it was a bitter disappointment.

It was then announced that Tszyu would be facing the high volume, hard punching, undefeated, IBF junior middleweight world champion, Bakhram Murtazaliev in Orlando, Florida in October.

Unbelievably, Tszyu was going into the fight as a big favourite, even though he was the challenger. I had followed the Chechen, Russian fighter for years and I knew he was going to be a very tough man to beat. He had a tremendous machine-like jab, with little defence but I knew that he never stops coming forward, and he could punch.

In the fight, Tszyu and Murtazaliev met in the centre of the ring and threw heavy shots in the first round. Hard thudding punches echoed around the ring as the champion connected with hooks as he doubled up with his jab in the second round.

Tszyu kept coming forward, landing big punches that seemed to bounce off the Russian. Tszyu was pressing forward but he was caught with a big left hook that put him down. He got up and fought back bravely but was caught by another left hook that knocked him to the canvas. Tszyu was hurt and on unsteady legs, but he got to his feet and fought on courageously, but Murtazaliev was picking him off with a steady arsenal that sent Tszyu down for a third time in the round. Tszyu received the standing eight count then the bell rang. Murtazaliev came out in the third round sticking the jab out and throwing hooks around the guard of the damaged Tszyu. The champion caught Tszyu with a perfect left hook that sent him down. Tszyu was up at the count of seven but was battered by a huge right hand that had him in serious trouble. Murtazaliev threw a volley of unanswered punches that forced the corner of Tszyu to throw in the towel in the third round. The jab and the power of the champion was too much.

Tszyu's people have always been there. Same crew that sweated in the gym with Kostya. Same crew that were by his side through thick and thin, through the spectacular wins to the bludgeoning defeats. They have been there forever, and they will always be there for him.

He will return and smile once more.

CAREER TOTALS

As of mid-2025, Tszyu has 25 wins (18 KOs) 2 losses 2 (1 KO)

"THERE'S NO SUCH THING AS AN EASY FIGHT. YOU HAVE TO GO THROUGH THE FIRE, NO MATTER HOW HOT IT IS".

TIM TSZYU

TIM TSZYU – A DAY IN THE LIFE

What time do you get up in the morning?

6:00 am.

Do you do your roadwork in the morning?

Yes. I run 8 kilometres, 4 times a week. I mix my training out with strength and conditioning.

Do you stretch your body?

A little. Not much.

What do you do after you run?

I do boxing exercises, I run backwards, forward sprints, explosive sprinting.

What do you have for breakfast?

I like an omelette and a bit of toast, electrolytes, water and my supplements.

What do you do after eating?

I always go for a 10-minute walk to help digestion. I come home and sleep.

How many days do you go to the gym?

6 days. Sunday is active recovery day. I go in the pool and sauna.

What is your favourite thing to do in the gym?

Sparring.

What time do you go to the gym?

If I'm sparring, I'll go at 11:00 am. If we are working on boxing and the technical aspects, I'll be in the gym at 2:00 pm. I always train for 2 hours.

Do you eat lunch?

Yes, I usually eat some lean chicken, rice, lean fish and some potatoes.

What do you have for dinner?

I have a chef who prepares my food and if we are in training camp, he stays with me. I'll eat chicken, rice fish potatoes vegetables but slightly bigger portions. I drink electrolytes and water.

Do you have a hobby or what do you do for fun?

I like cars. I like sports. If I'm playing basketball, soccer, or Pickle ball, it has to be competitive. I like going into the sauna and plunge pool and I enjoy having a BBQ and watching the boxing on the TV.

Did you have a job?

Yes. I worked in a factory that made fruit juice. Packing boxes. I worked shift work.

What time do you go to sleep?

I go to bed at 9:00 pm.

NON-SPARRING DAYS

- Warm up wrists and hands / Wrap / Tape hands.
- Warm up.
- Active Stretching.
- Foam Roller.
- Push ups x 50.
- Skipping 10 minutes – nonstop.
- Shadow box 4 x rounds x 4-minutes with a 30-second break in between.

Tszyu also does Shadow Boxing with 1kg dumbbells and 1/2 Kg dumbbells.

- Focus mitts 10 x rounds x 4-minutes with a 30-second break in between each round.
- Floor to ceiling bag / Double end bag 2 x rounds x 4-minutes with a 30-second break in between.
- Speed Bag 2 x rounds x 4-minutes with a 30-second break in between.
- Tszyu puts on a weighted vest.
- Skipping 5 minutes nonstop.
- Abdominal / stomach work.
- Sit-ups.
- Crunches.
- Leg raises.
- Side to side.
- Roller.
- Ball slams standing up.
- Medicine ball throws against wall.
- Juggling 2 balls (to balance and hand eye coordination)
- While standing up Tszyu waits on his coach, who has placed 5 coins on a board. His coach throws the coins up in the air and Tszyu has to quickly grab all 5 coins. (to test reflexes)

SPARRING DAYS

Tuesdays and Thursdays

- Warm up wrists and hands.
- Wrap / Tape hands.
- Warm up / active stretching.
- Shadow Boxing 2 rounds x 4-minutes – light pace with a 30-second break in between.
- Heavy Bag 1 round x 4-minutes – light steady pace.
- Sparring Begins.
- Sparring 10 rounds x 3:30 minutes with a 30-second break in between each round.
- Depending on the training camp, the Sparring rounds increase to 12 rounds x 3:30 minutes to then progress to 14 rounds to reach a maximum of 14 rounds x 3:30 minute rounds with 30-second breaks.
- Floor to ceiling bag 1 round x 3 minutes.
- Shadow boxing 1 round x 3 minutes.
- Skipping 3 minutes total.
- Abdominal / stomach exercises.
- Sit ups.
- Side to sides.
- Leg raises.
- Crunches.
- Stretching 10 minutes.

Tszyu punches downwards into a bed of steel balls alternating to toughen his nerves and the knuckles.

CASSIUS BALOYI

'The Impossible Dream'

BIOGRAPHY

Cassius Baloyi was born in 1974, in Malamulele, Limpopo, South Africa. Living and growing up in an impoverished village, with high unemployment, social unrest, crime and with little hope to grasp on to, Baloyi would run to school and learn to read and write and he would play in the heat and the dust until it was time to go home.

As day turned to night, the village would come alive with people cooking on wood fires, telling stories, and staring up at the brilliant bright stars above and praying to the heavens for a better day tomorrow.

When Baloyi was seven years old, his mother passed away, leaving his father to take care of his family and also go to work as a police officer to provide for them.

With a heavy heart, Baloyi's father Eric took Cassius to the local community clubhouse where he would learn how to box, and as the years passed, he would compete in two hundred amateur contests, with only three losses.

When I spoke to Baloyi about his years fighting in the amateurs, he said, "I was always a very quiet boy. All I wanted to do was box and my dream was to go to the Olympics in Barcelona and represent my people and make them proud. I was boxing well but they didn't take me. I don't know why. I kept going and fought hard and I became a World champion."

Baloyi was fighting an opponent he couldn't see. He was fighting an unbeatable foe. For Cassius, his dream was taken from him, but he fought on to right the unrightable wrong in the years that followed.

Baloyi turned professional in 1994, boxing in Las Vegas, Atlantic City, Glasgow, Manchester, and South Africa, racking up an unbeaten fourteen fight record to put him in line to fight for the WBU Super Bantamweight world title against the experienced Frankie Toledo in Florida. Baloyi won by a unanimous decision in 1996.

Baloyi would continue as an undefeated champion, fighting the Hungarian Southpaw, Laszlo Bognar, knocking him out in the seventh round to then move up in weight to face the experienced and durable Argentinian, Sergio Rafael Liendo in San Jose, for the vacant WBU featherweight world title, winning in a hard fought twelve round fight to take his second championship strap back to South Africa.

He travelled back to Scotland to knock out Brian Carr to then go back to South Africa and destroy Hector Lizarraga in one round. Baloyi packed his bags again, going to Wales to fight former WBO featherweight world champion, Steve Robinson in 2000. Robinson was known as 'The Cinderella Man' and he was a hero to the people of Wales, defending his world title seven times until he was outboxed by Naseem Hamed in 1995.

Baloyi boxed brilliantly to beat the proud Robinson and win by a majority decision.

In 2001, Baloyi would fight his friend from Limpopo, Philip Ndou in a fight that many thought they would see the big punching Ndou, knock out the WBU Super featherweight champion with ease but in the fight, Baloyi fought with pride, making it a close fight, but after twelve hard rounds he lost by a majority decision, losing his title and also an end to his 26 fight, unbeaten run.

Philip Ndou fought on, challenging Floyd Mayweather in his hometown of Grand Rapids for the 'Pretty Boy's WBC lightweight title in 2003, but he was knocked out in the seventh round. He would lose to Isaac Hlatshwayo in 2004, and Lovemore Ndou in 2009 on points in big fights in South Africa but he could never get back his glory days. For the man known as 'The Time Bomb', the clock ticked slowly. Ndou retired in 2016.

In 2002, Baloyi would fight the teak tough southpaw fighter from the Philippines, Tiger Ari. His real name was Eder Olivetti, and when he was born, his father named him after the Brazilian great, Eder Jofre, but he adopted Tiger Ari as his name in the ring. He would also use the name, Tiger Asakura when he fought in Japan.

The fight was held in Carnival City, South Africa and at stake was the vacant IBO Super Featherweight title.

Baloyi out boxed and broke down Ari, winning by TKO in the sixth round to become a three-time champion of the world.

Six months later, Baloyi faced the skilled technical boxer, Mbulelo Botile in Carnival City. Leading up to the fight, Botile had just lost his IBF featherweight title to Frankie Toledo in America, so he was desperate to beat Baloyi.

In the fight, Botile was boxing behind his superb jab, catching Baloyi and going to the body and head. Botile was in control until Baloyi enticed Botile to engage in a fist fight in the centre of the ring. Botile and Baloyi threw caution to the wind, with Baloyi connecting and hurting Botile with hard hooks and uppercuts that snapped his head back. Baloyi hit Botile with a barrage of punches that had him in trouble, and his legs betrayed him as he slumped to the canvas. Botile rose to his feet but was finished by a right hand in the eleventh round. Mbulelo Botile retired in 2005.

Baloyi continued winning, beating the 'Hands of Stone' Lehlo Ledwaba in a close and controversial decision in 2004. Baloyi made no mistake, five months later in the rematch, outboxing Ledwaba and winning by a unanimous decision in Brakpan. Lehlo Ledwaba retired in 2006 after a tremendous career, winning the WBU Bantamweight title, the IBF Super Bantamweight title, and the WBU featherweight title. He died from complications to COVID-19. Lehlo Ledwaba was forty-nine.

With no time to rest, Baloyi was back in the gym training to fight the undefeated boxer, Isaac Hlatshwayo.

The stylish South African known as 'The Angel' was twelve-round fighter, who had beaten Philip Ndou in 2004 and was seen by many as a future world champion. In the fight, Baloyi was outboxed by the bigger stronger man, losing his title by a unanimous points decision in August 2005.

Baloyi was then matched to face the experienced Mexican, Manuel Medina in Washington for the IBO and IBF Super featherweight world titles. Medina was coming to the end of a long gruelling career as a multiple World champion and he was seen as somewhat of a 'Dark Horse' – a spoiler and an extremely tough nut to crack, whenever he fought.

In the fight, Baloyi boxed brilliantly, knocking down the Mexican champion three times in the eleventh round, to win by a TKO and become a four-time champion of the world.

Two months later, Baloyi would lose his titles to the fast and stylish boxer from Guyana, Gairy St Clair. The man known as 'Superman' was a tough, experienced boxer who had been in training camps, sparring with Kostya Tszyu, and he also faced Diego Corrales and Amir Khan in recent years. Baloyi lost by a unanimous decision in South Africa in 2006.

Baloyi returned in early 2007, where he was matched to fight the Argentinian, Nazareno Gaston Ruiz for the vacant IBO Super Featherweight world title. Baloyi wasted no time, battering Ruiz in the third round to win and pick up his fifth world title.

Manuel Medina had beaten Kevin Kelley in late 2006 and the win warranted a rematch with Baloyi. The fight was held in South Africa, and it was a tight, messy affair with Medina being badly cut under his right eye from an accidental head butt which forced the contest to be stopped and officially ruled as a technical draw.

Baloyi, now in his thirteenth year as a professional, and with thirty-seven fights behind him, he was still chasing greatness.

In late 2007, he took on the challenge of the man who took his titles, Gairy St Clair, beating him by a unanimous decision at the Emperors Palace in South Africa.

In 2008, Baloyi fought the IBF Super featherweight world champion, Mzonke Fana.

Fana had beaten countryman Malcolm Klassen by a close split decision to become the IBF champion. In the fight, Baloyi used his boxing skills to outbox Fana to win by a majority decision and become the IBF Super Featherweight champion of the world and become a six-time world champion.

This would be Baloyi's last great night in the ring. Baloyi lost his world title to Malcolm Klassen, being stopped for the first time in his career in 2009. He kept fighting, losing to Mzonke Fana and Malcolm Klassen on points and he retired from the sport in 2012.

Cassius Baloyi went on a glorious quest, and he fought hard to become a six-time world champion in three different weight divisions. He can live in peace with himself knowing he lived the impossible dream.

CAREER TOTALS

37 wins (19 KOs), 8 losses (1 KO), 1 draw.

CASSIUS BALOYI – A DAY IN THE LIFE

What time did you get up in the morning?

I was up at 5:00 am every day.

Did you do your roadwork runs in the morning?

Yes. I would run 10 kilometres, with running at a good pace to alternate sprints with jogging.

Did you do any stretching before you started your run?

I didn't do any stretching at all until the early 2000s. I wish I would have earlier in my career.

What did you do after your roadwork?

I lived in the gym. My bed was there so I would go to the gym, and I would eat something, and I would rest and have a sleep.

What did you eat for breakfast?

I would eat eggs, bread, some tea and water.

What did you do after breakfast?

I would lie down and sleep.

What time did you go to the gym?

5:00 pm every day.

How many days did you train?

I trained 6 days. I did hard sparring, and we did 12 rounds of sparring on a Saturday. Sunday was a day off.

What was your favourite exercise in the gym?

I liked doing pull ups and stomach exercises – sit ups and crunches.

What time did you finish in the gym?

I trained for 2 hours, and I always finished at 7:00 pm.

What did you eat and drink after training?

Chicken, rice, tea and water. I couldn't cook but I tried to eat good. When I visited my father, I would eat salad and vegetables.

Did you have any hobbies or what did you do for fun?

I loved going to the movies. No hobbies, just boxing.

What job did you do?

I worked in a shop at the airport.

What time did you go to bed?

I slept in the gym, so there wasn't much to do so I went to sleep around 9:00 pm.

NON-SPARRING DAYS

- Warm up / light Stretch – 10 minutes.
- Jump Rope 10 minutes nonstop.
- Shadow Boxing 3 x 3-minute rounds. (1 minute break)
- (A total of 12 rounds x 3 minutes on the bags, all with a 1-minute break between rounds.)
- 4 x 3 minutes – Heavy Bag.
- 4 x 3 minutes – Floor to Ceiling bag. (also known as Double end bag)
- 4 x 3 minutes – Speed bag.
- Stomach exercises / Abdominal core exercises.
- Sit ups x 100.
- Crunches x 100.
- Leg raises x 100.
- Side to side while standing up. 25 of each side.
- Push ups x 50.
- Pull ups / Chin ups x 50.

SPARRING DAYS

- Wrap hands.
- Warm up / Light Stretch.
- Jump Rope – 10 minutes non-stop.
- Shadow boxing – 3 rounds x 3 minutes with a 1-minute break between each round.
- Start hard Sparring. 9–12 rounds with 3 different Sparring partners.
- Total of 12 rounds of Sparring with a 1-minute break in between each round.
- Stomach exercises. Abdominal / Core exercises.
- Sit ups x 100.
- Crunches x 100.
- Leg raises x 100.
- Side to sides while standing up. 25 of each side.
- Push ups x 50.
- Pull ups / Chin ups x 50.

*Always Sparred 12 hard rounds on Saturday.

adidas
J. OPETAIA

JAI OPETAIA

'The Weapon'

BIOGRAPHY

Jai Opetaia was born in Sydney, Australia in 1995. Born into a family with a proud Samoan and European heritage, Opetaia started kick boxing as a young boy of eight years old before he started to dedicate himself and his life to boxing.

With an amateur record of 138 fights with 15 losses, Opetaia was, at 16 years of age, the youngest boxer ever to earn selection to represent Australia, going to the 2012 Olympics in London. In 2014, the 6'2 southpaw competed in the Commonwealth Games in Glasgow, Scotland as a heavyweight.

As I walked into the deserted gym, I could hear grunts and there was echoes of battered leather bouncing off every wall. Opetaia was hammering the heavy bag and puddles of sweat from hard work and pain followed him as he moved in and out.

Everything was done correctly, and Opetaia was somewhere else, where nothing else mattered to him as he worked like a machine, drilling and grinding itself to exhaustion.

When I talked to Opetaia he was so focused, so determined to succeed and be better than the day before, saying to me "I work hard every day to be the best. I have to do it. There is nothing else for me and I am doing this for my family. I push myself in the gym, so I know when I go into battle, I'm more than ready and capable of overcoming anything in the ring. I see myself this way. Every day, I'm strengthening the sword, and I'm sharpening the sword. I am a weapon."

With 25 fights and 19 KOs, the twenty-nine-year-old Opetaia has proved he is the best Cruiserweight in the World.

Opetaia turned professional in August 2015, where he quickly established himself as a young dominant, power punching force at 200 pounds.

In 2022, he fought the experienced fighter and Latvian champion Mairis Briedis for the IBF Cruiserweight championship of the world. The fight was held in Australia's Gold Coast and for Opetaia, this was a huge step up in class and it was going to be the toughest test of his career thus far.

Briedis was a former Policeman and kick boxer who had only lost once since turning professional in 2009, losing by a majority decision to the outstanding Ukrainian southpaw, Oleksandr Usyk in 2018.

Going into the fight with Opetaia, he had beaten Danny Williams, Marco Huck, and Krzysztof Glowacki and he became the first boxer from Latvia to win a world title, beating

Mike Perez for the WBC cruiserweight title in his hometown of Riga in 2017. Briedis had also held the IBF, and WBO titles in recent years.

In the fight, Briedis was going to the body of Opetaia and lunging in with vicious uppercuts that found the target, breaking the Australia fighter's jaw in the second round. Opetaia fought bravely, counterpunching Briedis, catching him with hurtful combinations, and breaking the champion down. In the tenth round, with Briedis needing something special, he hit Opetaia with a superb uppercut that had him badly hurt. With Opetaia's mouth open and jaw badly swollen, he dug deep and showed heart and courage and fought with an undeniable will to win, and he kept fighting through the shock and the pain while Briedis fought with great urgency, throwing big punches, trying to finish him off. Briedis won the championship rounds, but his late rally wasn't enough.

Jai Opetaia fought the fight of his life in a war of attrition to win by a unanimous decision to become the IBF Cruiserweight champion of the world.

Opetaia returned to the ring after fourteen months due to his badly broken jaw, and he faced the 6'7 unbeaten challenger from Manchester, England, Jordon Thompson (15 bouts, 15 wins, (12 KOs), 0 losses, 0 draws).

The thirty-year-old Thompson was a former promising tennis player before he turned to boxing in 2015. Opetaia showed little ring rust, blasting the Englishman out in four rounds.

Opetaia wasted no time fighting through the politics of the sport and being stripped of his IBF title for taking a big money fight in Saudi Arabia. He was matched to fight another English fighter on the biggest stage of all. His opponent was the unbeaten wins (17 with 7 KOs) Ellis Zorro. Opetaia destroyed him in one round.

It was then announced that Opetaia would be returning to the desert to face the man who broke his jaw in two places, Mairis Briedis and they would again be fighting for the IBF cruiserweight championship of the world.

In the fight, the stubborn and proud champion Briedis, came out strong, targeting Opetaia's body and throwing strong punches to the Australian's chin to remind him he was in for another tough night. Opetaia fought with an iron fist and a calm maturity, boxing his way into a strong lead, breaking the Latvian hard man's nose in the sixth round. With blood pouring down his face and into his mouth, Briedis fought bravely, chasing and pressing to fight his way back into the later rounds, hurting Opetaia with a superb uppercut in the tenth round that damaged his nose and turned the tide in this gruelling contest, but even though Briedis won the championship rounds, Opetaia had done enough in the fight to win on points and become a two time world champion.

Next up was Jack Massey. Known as 'One Smack'. He had a record of wins (22 with 2 losses). Massey was defeated by Joseph Parker in 2023, and on the night, the 6'4 Englishman would be the bigger man. In the fight, Opetaia boxed brilliantly and threw hard accurate punches that broke down Massey, leaving his corner no choice but to throw in the towel in the sixth round in the desert of Riyadh, Saudi Arabia.

Opetaia started 2025 off with a bang, fighting at home and defending his title against the 6'6 New Zealand boxer, David Nyika. In the fight, Opetaia used his experience to find his range and patiently close in on the twenty-nine-year-old amateur star to overwhelm Nyika with relentless pressure as the rounds went by.

After throwing a thunderbolt right hand uppercut, early in the round, Nyika dropped to the canvas to then rise and succumb to a combination of hard right and left hooks that sent him into shock to then be finished off with a left hand that knocked him out cold in the fourth round in the Gold Coast of Australia.

Jai Opetaia is 27–0 with 21 stoppages and at twenty-nine years old, he has shown great bravery, skill, determination, speed and power to be the number one Cruiserweight champion in the sport of boxing.

He is a weapon.

CAREER TOTALS

As of mid-2025, Opetaia has 27 wins (21 KOs) with no losses and no draws.

"I KEEP PUSHING. I KEEP GOING. I PUSH THROUGH THE PAIN AS I WANT TO SHOW THE YOUNG KIDS THAT HARD WORK, SACRIFICE AND PHYSICAL AND EMOTIONAL PAIN CAN BE BEATEN."

JAI OPETAIA

JAI OPETAIA – A DAY IN THE LIFE

What time do you get up in the morning?
It varies for me. Around 7:00 am but it depends on my training.

Do you run in the morning?
I do. I run 10 kilometres once a week. I run 22 kilometres every now and then. I normally don't focus on long runs. I run, then sprint, recover, jog, run, sprint recover, and keep going until I'm exhausted. I also like to work out on air runners, skiers, to help with my cardio and conditioning.

Do you do any stretching?
yes, I do a lot of stretching. Stretching your whole body is very important to me. If I'm sore, I love stretching the muscles out. I also stretch a lot every night before I go to bed.

What do you do after your running workout?
I don't have breakfast. I have protein shakes at midday, and I drink water and electrolyte drinks. I then rest and relax until I go to the gym at 11am for my boxing session.

How many days do you train?
6 days, sometimes 7 days. For me, I'm like a sword. When the sword is made, it gets beaten, and it gets thrown into the fire to strengthen then it gets beaten, to then be sharpened. You strengthen the sword, then it gets sharpened. That is me. I love it and it's in my blood.

What time do you go to the gym?
I do 2 hours of boxing from 11am, working up to 15 rounds on heavy bag, shadow boxing and focus mitts. I then drink protein shakes and electrolytes and water.

What is your favourite exercise in the gym? I really like working in a group. Training very hard and going into deep waters in training. Everything has to be done. I also do ice baths, and I get massages, and I swim.

What time do you go back to the gym?
5:30 pm. This session is for strength training. Finish at 7:00 pm.

What do you eat and drink for dinner?
I eat around 7:30 pm. I eat good healthy foods. High protein. Meat, chicken, steaks, vegetables and salads. I like fish. I also drink water and protein shakes. I drink coconut water, and electrolyte drinks.

What do you do for fun, or do you have a hobby?
I love my family, and I love fishing. It's my life. Family, fighting and fishing.

What did you do for a job?
I worked in a shoe shop. I was 15 and I was working on a building site as a labourer.

What time do you go to sleep?
11:30 pm.

NON-SPARRING DAYS

- 9:30 am Daily Fitness Session.
- Circuit training is 45 minutes non-stop – 10 different Stations to be done – hard and fast until 45 minutes are over.
- Ropes (45 seconds each)
- Runner.
- Bench press light weights.
- Ball slams on ground.
- Push ups.
- Assault bike – hard and fast.
- Skiers machine – pull downs.
- Rowing machine.
- Box jumps.
- Burpees.
- Rest and Relax.
- 11:00 am Boxing Session Daily.
- Heavy Bag work x 3 minutes with 30-second break.
- 1 minute on Heavy Bag throwing hard fast straight punches.
- 1 minute throwing hard fast hooks.
- 1 minute throwing head and body combinations.
- 1 minute throwing hooks.
- 1 minute throwing combinations (Repeat twice)
- 3 rounds x 3 minutes throwing combinations of:
- Straight power punches.
- Tap-Tap – head body shots.
- Hard head punching followed by uppercuts.
- Shadow Boxing 4 rounds x 3 minutes to finish.

Monday Afternoons

- Heavy Weight explosive training.
- Closer to the fight, reduce to lighter weight.
- 2 ice baths a week.
- 2 massages a week.
- Swimming in the pool once per week – swim 20 x 25 metres.
- Full body stretching every night before going to bed.

SPARRING DAYS

Sparring is twice a week.

- Wrap / tape hands.
- Warm up / move around / Stretching / Shadow Box 25 minutes non-stop.

Sparring begins-

- 2 Sparring partners on rotation of every 2 rounds.
- Hard and fast sparring 8 rounds x 3 minutes progressing to 10 rounds to go 12 rounds non-stop.

GUILTY

MANUEL MEDINA

'A Warrior's Spirit'

BIOGRAPHY

Manuel Medina was born in the small coastal town of Tecuala, Mexico in 1971.

Life was always going to be tough for Medina, but he knew if he worked hard, he could live his life and things would get better for him, his grandmother who raised him and his family.

The twelve-year-old Medina would rise early and work doing anything to survive, unloading trucks all day in the sun and running errands for the truck drivers along the streets until dusk.

At night when the sun went down, he would walk up through the winding sandy path, dodging the cacti, to the ridge at the top of the hill and look at the fires that lit up the neighbouring shacks in the distance like fireflies dancing in the night. He would sit there thinking about what tomorrow would bring.

Medina started boxing as a young boy, fighting in fifty amateur contests, losing fourteen.

He would fight anyone and soon, it became his life, his survival and as time went by, it was a way to pay for his family members to go to school.

Medina turned professional in 1985, just barely turning fourteen years old, fighting grown men for a fistful of dollars in Tijuana, Culiacan, and San Diego.

When I asked 'Mantecas' about his decision to turn professional at such a young age, he said, "Our lives were tough, but I always told myself that everything can happen with hard work. I could fight and I was never afraid of hard work. I wanted to accomplish. Boxing made me grow as a person and I knew I was helping my family."

Medina settled in the turbulent border town of Tijuana, and he worked all day to then go to the gym, sparring anyone he could, facing hardened hungry fighters that were all desperate to fight for the chance of a better life or a way out of the barrios.

Medina fought in thirty-nine fights, grinding out and beating down his opponents with his relentless pressure and wild two-fisted attacks, losing three contests until 1991. He beat the talented Tyrone Jackson and the experienced Steve Cruz in 1990 in hard fought points victories that put him in line to fight for the IBF featherweight championship of the world.

Cruz had ripped the WBA featherweight title from the Irish strongman, Barry McGuigan, in the heat of Las Vegas in 1986 and he had also beaten Tracy Harris Patterson to then lose to Jorge Paez on points in 1989.

Troy Dorsey was the newly crowned IBF featherweight champion, and he was a former three-time kick boxing champion before turning to boxing.

The Texas hard man had fought Tom Johnson, twice and he challenged the exciting showman, Jorge Paez twice in 1990 for his featherweight titles, losing on points in a fight of the year battle in the February and then taking the champion to a draw five months later in a gruelling battle of attrition of blood and guts. Dorsey then fought Alfred Rangel for the vacant IBF featherweight title in June 1991, knocking him out in the first round to realise his dream.

Leading up to the fight, Medina trained hard, sparring with three different sparring partners up to sixteen hard rounds every day in camp, as he knew Dorsey was a two-fisted body puncher who relied on his strength and toughness to win. Medina knew there would be no finesse, no technique, just unyielding pressure and courage from the twenty-eight-year-old champion.

In the fight, Dorsey came out hard, knocking Medina down in the second and third rounds with right hands, but Medina recovered quickly to fight his way back into the fight, counter punching with accurate left jabs and lunging right hands. As the fight went on, Medina used his tremendous footwork and a two-fisted non-stop body attack, that forced Dorsey to drop his hands, leaving himself open to be bust up to the head. The brave champion kept coming forward, but Medina was throwing slashing punches that opened up cuts to both of his eyes.

With blood pouring down his face, Dorsey never took a backward step but in the end, despite the two knockdowns, Manuel Medina used his superb stamina and superior boxing skills to become a world champion in 1991 at twenty years old.

Troy Dorsey fought on until 1998, facing Kevin Kelley, Jesse James Leija, Calvin Grove, Oscar De La Hoya Jesus Chavez and Gabriel Ruelas.

Medina took no time to celebrate his victory and three months later, he took on the challenger, Tom 'Boom Boom' Johnson (26 wins, 1 loss,1 draw) in Los Angeles. In a close fight, Medina won on points after the referee stopped the action in the ninth round, asking the doctor to look at the cut that was caused by an accidental head clash that opened up Medina's left eye. The doctor deemed the damage was too great for the fight to continue. It was an unsatisfactory end to a well-matched fight.

Medina then travelled to Europe, fighting in France and Italy, winning on points in hard fought contests.

Tom Johnson followed Medina to Melun in France to challenge the Mexican champion in 1993, and after a tough close fight, Johnson won by a split decision to become the IBF featherweight champion of the world.

The loss was a turning point for Medina. With almost fifty fights behind him, and years of training and fighting, he could have called it a day but the warrior spirit in him made him continue.

Medina fought on in long hard fights, winning and losing but he never gave up and his will to win was always there.

In 1995, he pounded out a split decision win, over Alejandro Gonzales, to become a two-time featherweight champion of the world to then travel to Tokyo, Japan to face the challenge of Luisito Espinosa in his first defence and lose his title on points. Medina then travelled to Dublin, Ireland to face the brash and cocky WBO featherweight champion from Sheffield, Naseem Hamed. Medina was seen as cannon fodder for the 22 win, no losses knockout artist who had destroyed the world champion and pride of Wales, Steve Robinson, ripping his title away to become a boxing superstar in 1995.

In the bout, Medina gave Hamed a tremendous fight, catching him and stunning the twenty-one-year-old with a two-fisted attack that gave him a lot to think about. Hamed's awkward style and power eventually came to fruition, knocking the Mexican down three times and with Medina's eyes badly swollen, and finding it hard to see, he kept coming forward throwing punches until the ringside doctor called a halt to the fight at the end of the eleventh round. Medina sat exhausted on his stool – the fight was Hamed's.

It was now 1997, and Medina challenged the WBC featherweight champion, Luisito Espinosa for the chance to win back his old title. The fight was held in Manila and in a messy affair, Espinosa kept his title with a technical decision in the eighth round due to suffering a cut to his right eye by an accidental head butt.

Medina returned from the Philippines and with no rest, he immediately fought the southpaw, Derrick Gainer in Mashantucket, where he was knocked out by a big left hand in the ninth round. Two months later, he beat Jose Ayala to then challenge the experienced IBF featherweight champion, Hector Lizarraga, in San Jose. Medina beat the champion by a hard-fought unanimous decision, winning his third world championship against all the odds. After a well-deserved vacation to rest and enjoy life Mantecas travelled to Hull in England to fight Paul Ingle (21 wins,1 loss). With both fighters going toe to toe in a tremendous fight, Ingle decked Medina three times in the fight, to then find himself cut and badly hurt, going down in the twelfth round to hang on and win by a unanimous points victory in 2000.

This fight could have been the end for Medina in an unforgiving sport of kings and crooks, but it was just another chapter, and it was yet another turning point in the Mexican's fifteen-year career.

Medina returned and beat the southpaw, Frankie Toledo on points in Las Vegas to go on another winning streak, challenging for his fourth world title in 2001. Frankie Toledo stood in his way, but Medina made no mistake, battering the champion from New Jersey, and forcing his corner to end the onslaught in the fifth round to win back the IBF crown.

Medina could have fought anyone, but he took on the talented Johnny Tapia and once again, he lost his title in his first defence. In 2003, Medina fought the tremendously talented boxer puncher, and fellow Mexican, Juan Manuel Marquez and was overpowered and outboxed and stopped in the seventh round in Las Vegas.

Unbelievably, Medina came back yet again, winning twice in four months to then get the call to travel to Scotland to fight the proud and determined WBO featherweight champion, Scott Harrison. The tough, no-nonsense Scot was making his third defence of the title he won by beating Julio Pablo Chacon in 2002. He defended his newly won title against Wayne 'The Pocket Rocket' roving too strong at the weight for the Irishman in a great fight in Glasgow.

In the lead up to the Medina fight, Harrison would run up the Scottish highlands, in the mountains with heavy back packs on him, while Medina sweated it out in Tijuana.

In the fight, with everything against him, and thousands of proud Scottish fans singing and dancing, the Mexican walked to the ring focused on the task in front of him. Harrison walked out; stone faced with no emotion.

In the fight Harrison came forward using pressure as his weapon, but he was counter-punched by the awkward two-fisted combination punches of Medina.

Medina fought his fight, never letting the champion get set. Harrison was aggressive but he was frustrated and was trying to take the Mexican out with wild hooks while Medina boxed and moved until the final bell. In the end, Manuel Medina outboxed Harrison to win by a split decision to become a five-time world champion at the same weight. Medina shared this fantastic achievement with one of the greatest fighters and pound for pound elites in the history of the sport, Sugar Ray Robinson.

Medina returned to Scotland four months later to fight Harrison in a rematch, and he was knocked down three times in the fight to then be knocked down a fourth time in the eleventh round to end the fight at the Braehead Arena. The courageous Medina succumbed to the aggressive pressure and onslaught of a desperate man who had to win.

After 75 fights and many battles behind him, Medina should have retired but at thirty-two he carried on – training, sparring, running, and fighting.

After more wins, and losses against Cassius Baloyi, Kevin Kelley, and Malcolm Klassen, Manuel Medina retired in 2008. He realised his dreams, and he achieved greatness on a long rocky road. He fought with courage and heart every time he stepped through the ropes, and he did so with a warrior's spirit.

CAREER TOTALS

Medina finished his career with a 67 wins (32 KOs), 16 losses (8 KOs) and 1 draw.

"I GAVE EVERYTHING. I FOUGHT HARD FOR MYSELF AND FOR MY FAMILY. I AM HAPPY."

MANUEL MEDINA

MANUEL MEDINA – A DAY IN THE LIFE

What time did you get up in the morning?

5:00 am.

Did you run in the morning?

Yes. I ran 10 kilometres in 45 minutes, every day.

Did you stretch your body before you run?

Yes. I stretched my back, my legs, my stomach and my arms and shoulders.

What did you do after running?

I shadow boxed for 4 x 3-minute rounds.

What did you eat for breakfast?

Beans, 2 eggs, some sausage.

What did you do after eating?

I would visit my family, have a rest and sleep until midday. I would eat a good lunch of chicken, or fish and salads, orange juice and water.

What time did you go to the gym?

I would train from 3:00 pm every day. I would finish training at 5:30 pm.

What was your favourite exercise in the gym?

I loved warming up. It was a great feeling and a good sensation.

How many days did you train?

6 days. Sunday off.

What did you eat and drink for dinner?

I only had a sandwich, maybe fish and salad. Some water and juice. I ate light meal at around 6:30 pm.

What did you do for fun?

I loved riding my bike. I also enjoyed scuba diving.

Did you have a job?

Yes. My job was unloading 2,500 boxes of papaya fruit from a truck on to a loading dock. It was hard work, but I had no choice.

What time did you go to sleep?

8:30 pm.

NON-SPARRING DAYS

- Warm up, stretching and moving – 15 minutes.
- 6 rounds x 3 minutes on Heavy Bag with a 1-minute break between each round.
- 3 rounds x 3 minutes on the Double End Bag with 1-minute break after each round.
- 2 rounds x 3 minutes on the Speed Bag with 1-minute break after each round.
- 2 rounds x 3 minutes Skipping non-stop.
- 2 rounds x 3 minutes Shadow Boxing non-stop.
- Sit ups x 100.
- Medina would relax in the Jacuzzi and the sauna.
- Medina would swim in the ocean, and he would scuba dive every 20 days for 1 hour under the water for his endurance.

SPARRING DAYS

- Wrap hands.
- Warm up / Stretching/ Moving was 15 minutes.
- Skipping 15 minutes non-stop.
- Shadow Boxing 3 rounds x 3 minutes with a 1-minute break.
- 10–12 rounds of Sparring x 3-minute rounds with a 1-minute break at the end of each round.
- There was always 4 or 5 Sparring partners waiting to engage in hard Sparring.
- 2 rounds x 3 minutes on Double End Bag. Non-stop.
- Sit ups x 100.

WBC
WBC

JESSIE JAMES LEIJA

'The Texas Tornado'

BIOGRAPHY

James Leija was born in San Antonio, Texas in 1966 – a city steeped in history and home of the famous 'Battle of the Alamo' where Texas fought for its independence from Mexico in 1836.

Leija initially took up boxing to get physically fit and strong with the thought of becoming a firefighter or a policeman.

He was nineteen years old when he walked through the doors of the gym. His father Jesse had been a boxer and through time, he could see that his son had the discipline, and the talent, needed to be a fighter. Leija campaigned as an amateur, boxing in 28 fights with 5 losses, to then turn professional.

Leija took his father's first name and stepped into the ring as Jesse James Leija in 1988.

Leija had a record of 21 fights with 1 draw, when he was matched to fight the 1984, Olympic flyweight gold medallist, Steve McCrory in 1991.

McCrory was a talented, stylish boxer who had trained out of the 'Kronk' gym in Detroit.

Leija won by a unanimous points decision. McCrory retired shortly after, and he died in 2000 at the age of thirty-six.

In 1993, the unbeaten Leija faced the experienced fighter from Phoenix Arizona, Louie Espinoza, who had been fighting for eleven years as a professional and he had won the WBA Bantamweight world title in 1987, and the WBO Featherweight Championship in 1989.

Leija won well by a unanimous points decision.

Azumah Nelson was the WBC Super Featherweight world champion and Leija was 26 wins 0 losses and 1 draw and the number three contender for his title. The fight was on the undercard to Julio Cesar Chavez v Pernell Whitaker at 'The Alamodome' in San Antonio, Texas.

Nelson had been fighting in tough battles around the world for fifteen years, facing Salvador Sanchez, Wilfredo Gomez, Marcos Villasana, Mario Martinez, Pernell Whitaker, Juan Laporte, Gabriel Ruelas and Jeff Fenech, just to name a few and he wasn't done just yet.

Nelson arrived in San Antonio, four weeks early to train for his tenth defence of his title and Leija and him worked out at the same gym, albeit different times. Nelson had experienced and faced everything in his long career. He knew every trick in the book, and he was a master of mind games.

In the build up to the fight, he asked his people to ask Leija if he wanted to do some sparring with him so Leija could get an insight into what a beating he was going to take in the fight.

In the fight, with 60,000 people cheering and rooting for their native son Leija, Nelson came out for his twentieth world championship fight, slow and steady, jabbing, while Leija was showing his own quick jab. Nelson was stalking and he was landing crisp hard shots to Leija. It was a battle for control, with both fighters using their jabs in a close fight. In the twelfth round, Nelson finished brilliantly, and he boxed and moved and hit Leija with accurate punches to win the round. In the end, the fight was scored a split decision draw and Nelson retained his title.

Leija and Nelson would meet again in the rematch in Las Vegas and Leija would fight better, pouring on the pressure in the final rounds, to beat him on points, and take Nelson's belt and become the WBC Super Featherweight champion of the world.

With little time to celebrate his historic victory, Leija took a vacation and on his return it was announced he would be making his first defence against the tough Mexican, Gabriel Ruelas.

Leija had seven weeks to prepare, and he had to boil himself down in training, plus go on a deficit, 1,100 calories-a-day diet.

Leija made the weight, but his body was drained.

In the fight, Ruelas targeted the body of Leija, with Leija throwing his jab and coming forward. The Mexican hit Leija with a body punch that made him go backwards, and Ruelas threw a huge right uppercut between the guard of the champion, catching him perfectly under the jaw, sending him down hard in the second round. Leija bravely rose to his feet and survived. The fight would go the distance. Ruelas was the better, sharper boxer, but it was the body shots that took the legs from Leija that set up the second knockdown in the twelfth round that sealed the win for Ruelas in Las Vegas.

It was now 1995, and Oscar De La Hoya was 19-0 and the WBO lightweight world champion and Jesse James Leija decided to move up in weight to challenge the 1992 Olympic Gold medallist from Los Angeles.

In the fight, 'The Golden Boy' was defending his title for the sixth time, and he wasted no time battering the smaller Leija, hitting him with fast jabs and hard hooks, and a superb left hook, which forced Leija's father no choice but to throw the towel in to save his son from further punishment in the second round at Madison Square Garden.

Leija moved back down in weight to challenge Azumah Nelson for his WBC Super Featherweight title.

In the fight, Nelson walked to the ring smiling, followed by his entourage, banging African drums and chanting. The champion came out, stalking Leija, with Nelson attacking the body with hard punches, to then knock Leija down in the first round with a huge right hand. The Texan showed a huge heart, getting up, when others would have stayed down. Nelson continued to systematically break down Leija with an onslaught of punches until the referee stepped in, stopping the fight in the sixth round. When I asked Leija about the fight, he said, "After the first-round knockdown, I can't remember a thing. I was fighting on instinct. Nothing else."

Leija came back, winning six fights in a row, to then fight Azumah Nelson for a record, fourth time in San Antonio in 1998.

The fight was staged at 'The Alamodome' for the vacant IBA lightweight world title.

In the fight, it was a battle of the jabs, but Leija was sharper, showing lateral movement and side to side, stick and move tactics. Nelson broke his hand in the fifth round leaving Leija to box to a unanimous points win.

Azumah Nelson retired after the fight, to then return ten years later to fight Jeff Fenech in a charity match up in Australia.

Leija fought on and four months later, he challenged the IBF lightweight champion of the world, Shane Mosley. Leija took the fight on three weeks' notice and going into the fight, he had to lose seventeen pounds in twenty-one days to make the weight.

In the fight, Leija fought with heart and never stopped coming forward to fight, but the undefeated champion, Mosley was too strong and fast, throwing accurate combinations and knocking Leija down and out punching him, and picking him off until the end of the ninth round, with his father telling the referee it was over.

Leija never gave up and from there, he would fight in six fights, losing once to Juan Lazcano in a controversial split decision.

In late 2000, he beat the talented and tough Ivan Robinson on points, also knocking him down in the eighth round to secure the victory in Las Vegas.

He fought the undefeated 32-0 Puerto Rican Hector Camacho Jnr. in his fiftieth fight which was eventually ruled as a no contest due to Camacho being unable to continue after an accidental head clash caused a cut above his right eye.

Leija would then fight Micky Ward in Texas at 140lbs. Ward had been in tough hard-fought wars, fighting Emanuel Augustus, Antonio Diaz, Shea Neary and Zab Judah, and Leija thought he had enough in him to outwork and beat the man from Lowell Massachusetts.

In a fast-paced fight, Leija boxed brilliantly, going to the body and head of Ward, with Ward never taking a backward step, throwing wide overhand right hands, and uppercuts on the inside. There was an accidental head butt in the first round that caused a large cut over Leija's right eye, but he kept fighting on the inside, while Ward was effective, picking his punches from a distance. In the fourth round, both fighters were having great success going to the body and it seemed that Ward was using his brute strength to get back into the fight. In the fifth round, Ward was pushing Leija back and he was trying to impose his will on to Leija as his eye was pouring blood. As the two warriors sat on their stools, the referee stopped the fight due to the damage to Leija's eye and the fight went to the scorecards. Leija was ahead on points, and he won by a technical decision.

Micky Ward went on to fight Arturo Gatti for thirty action packed rounds in one of the greatest trilogies in the history of boxing. He retired in 2003.

Leija travelled to Australia to face the dangerous Russian, Kostya Tszyu for his Super Lightweight WBC, IBF and WBA titles and in the fight, Leija was boxing well on the inside, while Tszyu was trying to find his range. As the fight went on, Tszyu was hurting Leija to the body with thudding punches. In the six round, Tszyu was pressing forward and hitting Leija to the body and head with hard blows to end the round. The fight was stopped as Leija sat on his stool, due to a perforated right ear injury.

Leija fought on, winning his next four fights and beating the young sensation, Francisco Bojado, on a split decision.

Jesse James Leija fought Arturo Gatti for his WBC light welterweight title in his final fight at the age of thirty-eight years old, losing by knockout in the fifth round in Atlantic City.

After fifty-seven fights, with his father by his side, it was time. Leija fought with heart, and he gave his all in the ring to become champion of the world and a hero to millions of Texans.

CAREER TOTALS

47 wins (19 KOs), 7 losses (5 KOs) and 2 draws.

JESSIE JAMES LEIJA – A DAY IN THE LIFE

What time did you get up in the morning?

7:00 am every day.

Did you run in the morning?

Yes. 8:00 am.

How far did you run?

I ran 9 Miles a day. I did interval running workout drills also, which was working on my speed. I would run around the track twice at a fast pace. I would jog, sprint, jog, run hard and fast. 7 to 8 weeks out from the fight, I would do interval drills plus run 4 to 5 miles.

Did you stretch out?

I wasn't a big stretcher. I did a light stretch.

What did you do after running?

I would go into the whirlpool and sauna for around 30 minutes, then I would go home and eat breakfast.

What did you eat for breakfast?

Scrambled eggs, high protein, oatmeal, orange juice.

What did you do after breakfast?

I would rest my body and relax until it was time to go to the gym.

What time did you go to the gym?

I would get to the gym at 4:00 pm and train for 3 hours.

How many days did you train?

I trained hard for 6 days. Sometimes 7 days if it was close to the fight. I always trained hard so I knew I could give everything I could in the fight.

What was your favourite exercise in the gym?

I liked hitting the double-end bag for my timing and speed.

What did you eat for dinner?

I enjoyed chicken breast. Vegetables. I liked pasta, and red meat for high protein.

What did you do for fun or a hobby?

I am a family man. My wife and kids. I love playing golf. I'm pretty good at golf. I play off of an 11 handicap.

Did you have a job?

I worked in a potato chip factory but at eighteen years old I was boxing.

What time did you go to bed?

11:30 pm.

NON-SPARRING DAYS

Monday, Wednesday and Friday

- Wrap hands.
- Warm up body / moving around – 10 minutes.
- Shadow Boxing 15 minutes non-stop.
- Double End Bag 4 rounds x 3 minutes with a 1-minute break between each round.
- Focus Mitts 4 rounds x 3 minutes with a 1-minute break between each 3-minute round. This was all about focusing on a game plan, what combinations would work on his opponent, and perfecting the technique.
- Hit the Heavy Bag 4 rounds x 3-minute rounds with a 1-minute break between each round.
- Jump Rope 15 minutes non-stop.

Abdominal Exercises

- Sit ups.
- Leg raises.
- Crunches.
- Side-to-sides while standing up.
- Medicine ball slams into stomach.
- Planks – holding straight.
- Stair master 20 minutes non-stop to finish workout.

SPARRING DAYS

Tuesday, Thursday and Saturday

- (7 weeks out from a fight)
- Wrap / Tape hands.
- Step into the ring in the gym.
- Shadow Box 15 minutes non-stop.
- Hit the Heavy Bag 2 rounds x 3 minutes non-stop.
- Sparring begins. 3 Sparring partners waiting to go. Depending on what stage in training camp but normally start from 4 rounds x 3 minutes with a 1-minute break between each round. Progress to 6 rounds to then do 10 rounds x 3 minutes.

Note: The mindset was, if you could do 10 hard rounds of sparring in the gym, you could do 12 rounds in the fight. You were ready.

- 1 week before the fight – no sparring.
- Double End Bag 3 rounds x 3 minutes with a 1-minute break.
- Jump Rope 10 minutes non-stop.
- Stair Master 30 minutes to finish workout.

WBC
BIKA

SAKIO BIKA

'The Sting of the Scorpion'

BIOGRAPHY

Sakio Bika was born in Douala, Cameroon in 1979.

Living and growing up with no running water, Bika played soccer in the dirt streets and went to school.

In a country which was plagued by drought and floods, life was hard in this under-developed land.

Bika was eleven years old when the Cameroon soccer team reached the quarter finals of the 1990 World Cup. There were children from the slums of Douala, dancing in the street, and drums beating and hordes of people all huddled together, watching a TV propped up high on crates, all hoping to get a view of their hero's. Cameroon lost but they gave the people hope and something to believe in.

Bika loved playing soccer, and he was a very good player, until he was injured in a game. He hurt his knee, and he had no choice but to rest so he could get strong again.

He attended a school that had a big hall for the kids, which hosted basketball, badminton, soccer and boxing. There was a heavy bag, and a ring and Bika would go every day and sit and watch the other children playing and practicing. Bika was getting stronger, so he started punching the heavy bag for fun and after a while, he thought about being a boxer.

Bika started boxing at the age of fourteen, in 1993, and from there, he competed in 144 contests with 7 losses. He was an All-African champion, and he represented Cameroon in the Sydney 2000, Olympic games. He took the nickname of 'The Scorpion' after being stung by one when he was playing in the sand.

He turned professional immediately after the games, and when his teammates travelled home to central Africa, Bika stayed in Sydney.

Bika won his first ten fights, to then lose to the awkward spoiler, Sam Soliman in 2002.

The African stormed back with another ten victories, travelling to Osaka, Japan to face the popular Yoshihiro Araki for the vacant OPBF middleweight title. Bika was too aggressive and powerful for the Japanese fighter, stopping him in the tenth round. He travelled back to Japan for the rematch knocking Araki out in the fifth round.

In 2006, he would pack his bags again, and travel to Germany to challenge Markus Beyer for his WBC super-middleweight title. In the fight, Bika was the aggressor, and he was out punching the champion with his left jab and straight right hand. It was a chess match, and the crafty Kraut was happy to jab from his southpaw stance, and box and move. Bika stalked Beyer and in the fourth round, the African hit the German with a committed strong left jab, followed by a head butt that split open the champion's right eye. Time out was called, and the fight was stopped. Beyer kept his title on a technical decision. A rematch was agreed by Beyer, but it never eventuated.

Bika had shown he was a handful to anyone at 168 pounds, with his tough, rough, aggressive style. Mikkel Kessler's people asked Bika to come to Copenhagen, Denmark to help the WBA world champion prepare for Marcus Beyer in their unification match. Bika accepted and when he arrived at the gym, Kessler didn't want to spar him.

Five months later, Bika challenged the unbeaten (41 wins) Welshman, Joe Calzaghe for his world titles. It was a tear up, with The Scorpion coming forward and throwing everything at Calzaghe. The Welsh warrior was the better boxer, and he was more accurate, using his fast hands, trying to nullify Bika's wild hooks. Calzaghe was bruised and cut in a rough fight, also taking a few low blows in the heated battle.

In the end, Calzaghe won by a unanimous decision in Manchester.

In 2007, he fought the French Canadian, Lucian Bute in Quebec, for the IBF eliminator, losing on points.

Later that year, he won The Contender series, competition in America, beating Donny Mc Crary, Sam Soliman, and Jaidon Codrington in a wild final fight in Boston.

He returned to Australia and knocked out the tough Argentinian fighter, Gustavo Javier Kapusi in the first round with a body shot.

In 2008, he was off again, this time to fight Peter Manfredo Jnr., for the vacant IBO super middleweight world title in Manfredo's hometown of Rhode Island, Providence, New England. Manfredo had a great amateur career with 165 bouts, and since turning professional, he had shared the ring with Frankie Randall, Sergio Mora, Joe Calzaghe, and Jeff Lacy.

In the fight, Bika started slow, jabbing out with Manfredo moving tentatively throwing the jab, but wary of the African's power. Bika, looking like he was carved out of stone, was beating the twenty-seven-year-old 'Pride of Providence' with his stinging left jab followed up with a thudding right hand. Manfredo had his father in his corner and the crowd behind him, cheering his every move. Bika went down in the second round and although it wasn't a hard blow, Manfredo caught him off balance and the referee gave him the count. Bika protested to no avail, and finished the round, throwing wild and angry punches. In the third round, Bika caught Manfredo with twenty-one unanswered head punches on the ropes, leaving him stunned and crashing to the canvas. He got up quickly and Bika continued the onslaught to his body and head, finishing with a big right hook to end the fight.

Sakio Bika had achieved his dream of becoming Champion of the World.

In 2010, Bika was matched to fight the Frenchman, Jean Paul Mendy in an IBF super middleweight title eliminator. For Bika, winning would get him another chance to have a go at the IBF champion, Lucian Bute so everything was on the line.

In the fight, the undefeated, 28 wins, 0 losses and 1 draw, southpaw, Mendy was boxing in a slow start, happy to use his jab. Bika came out aggressive, with a sting in his tail, stalking and connecting with good combinations. He hit Mendy with a good left hook to the head that had him in trouble, following up with a flurry that sent him down. Animal killer instinct then took over with Bika throwing a vicious uppercut while Mendy was down. The Frenchman was hurt, and Bika was disqualified.

Bika returned four months later after getting the call on late notice to fight Andre Ward in his hometown of Oakland.

Once again, Bika would be fighting for a world title. Andre Ward was a gold medallist in the 2004 Olympic Games, and he was the WBA super middleweight champion of the world.

Ward was originally fighting Andre Dirrell in the Super Six tournament, but he pulled out after sustaining an injury in his training camp. The unbeaten champion had 120 amateur fights with only 5 losses, and since turning professional, his record stood at 22 wins with 0 losses and 13 KOs.

In the fight, Bika and Ward wrestled and clinched, with Ward happy to work on the inside, while Bika stepping back to try and land wild bombs to catch the champion. It was a rough, tough clash of styles, with low blows and head butts, making an ugly encounter that Ward won by a unanimous decision.

After a few wins, Bika travelled back to New York to fight the tough and durable Mexican, Marco Antonio Periban for the WBC super-middleweight championship title.

Bika walked to the ring with experienced trainer, Ronnie Shields, sporting a shaved African Mohawk, looking fired up and strong. The hard punching Mexican entered the ring unbeaten with a 20–0 record with 12 wins by knockout.

The Mexican fought with heart, but couldn't match the aggression and wild punching, two fisted attacks of Bika.

The Scorpion clubbed his way through Periban's guard, finishing stronger to win the fight by a majority decision in Brooklyn. Sakio Bika won the WBC super-middleweight title to become a two-time world champion in his thirty-ninth fight and in doing so, he became a hero to his people in Cameroon.

Bika could have fought anyone in his first defence, but he took on the unbeaten hard punching, 26–0, Anthony Dirrell from Flint, Michigan. The fight was at the Barclays Centre in Brooklyn, New York and the challenger, known as 'The Dog' was eager to bite the hand that fed him.

In the fight, Bika was the aggressor, but Dirrell was strong, taking the champions onslaught to come back with his own big right hands. Bika was coming in wild, while Dirrell was measuring him for the counter. In the fifth round, Dirrell hit Bika with a lightning fast, hard right hand that knocked Bika down. The African got up quickly and mauled his way back into the fight. It was a back-and-forth battle with Bika pouring on the pressure, throwing big thudding blows to the head and body of Dirrell.

In the eleventh round, Dirrell was hammering Bika with hard left hooks and Bika continued to bite down and throw wild, hard hooks to the body, catching Dirrell and sending him down. The referee warned the champion about his roughhouse tactics and seconds later, Bika had a point taken from him for going low. Dirrell was given five minutes to recover. The fight went the distance, and Bika retained his world title with a split-decision draw. The rematch was signed and eight months later, they met again at the LA Galaxy's 'Stub Hub' arena in Los Angeles.

Leading up to the fight, there was bad blood boiling from Dirrell. For Bika, it was part of boxing.

In the fight, Dirrell came out, intent on fighting fire with fire, being much more aggressive, throwing big punches at Bika. The champion came back, mauling his way in with hard thumping blows to Dirrell's head and body. It was a hard-fought battle with both fighters desperate to win. In the eighth round, Bika lost a point for a low blow, but he continued to fight wildly, with Dirrell counter punching and connecting with his own hard accurate combination punches until the final bell. Dirrell won the contest by a unanimous decision.

With the loss, Bika was still considered too much of a risk for anyone with a belt and with no one willing to risk what was theirs in the super middleweight division, Bika moved up to 175 lbs (79 kilos) to face arguably the best light heavyweight in the world – Adonis Stephenson.

The Haiti born, Canadian world champion was a hard punching southpaw, who was both controversial and unpopular to many. He was 25 wins with 1 loss, and he was fast, wild and a dangerous fighter.

In the fight, Stephenson controlled the fight with his southpaw jab, and big left hand. Bika fought hard but couldn't get close enough to be effective. Stephenson won well by a unanimous points decision in Quebec.

Bika returned to the ring twenty-seven months later in Australia as a super middleweight, winning twice, to then retire in 2017.

In his career, he fought them all in their own backyards. He won and he lost but whenever he fought, he always came to fight, and he gave them hell.

From the dirt and the sand of Douala to the Sydney Olympic Games, to New York and Atlantic City, and beyond, he realised his dream of being a World champion.

CAREER TOTALS

Bika finally hung the gloves up for good after the Soliman fight in 2021 with a career record of wins 35 (22 KOs), 7 losses and 3 draws.

"I FOUGHT EVERYONE I COULD IN THEIR BACKYARDS AND I DID MY BEST TO WIN EVERY TIME I FOUGHT."

SAKIO BIKA

SAKIO BIKA – A DAY IN THE LIFE

What time did you get up in the morning?

6:00 am.

Did you run in the morning?

Yes. I was a very good runner. I ran at a fast pace for 45 minutes every day. I only ran by time.

Did you stretch out before you run?

Yes. I stretched my body and legs for 20 minutes before I ran. I would go for a massage once every week.

What did you do after running?

I had breakfast, and I rested and slept for 2 hours.

What did you eat and drink for breakfast?

I had omelette, cereal, fruit yogurt, banana and watermelon. Juice and water.

What time did you go to the gym?

5:00 pm until 7:00 pm every day.

What was your favourite exercise in the gym?

I liked everything. It all had to be done.

What did you eat for dinner?

I liked pasta, sweet potatoes, vegetables and steak. I ate fish and rice a lot. I drank juice and water.

What did you do for fun or a hobby?

I love soccer and basketball. I go to the movies. I enjoy music and going to concerts. I love American comedy shows.

What job did you do?

I worked in farm markets. Up until I fought Joe Calzaghe, I worked as a glazier putting in windows.

What time did you go to sleep?

I would go to bed at 10:00 pm and be asleep by 11:00 pm.

NON-SPARRING DAYS

Tuesday and Thursday

- Stretching / Warm up / Moving around 15 minutes non-stop.
- Shadow Box 2 rounds x 3 minutes with a 30-second break between each round.
- Focus mitts 6 rounds x 3 minutes with a 30-second break between each round.
- Hit the Heavy Bag 4 rounds x 3 minutes with 30-second breaks between each round.
- Floor to ceiling bag / Double end bag 2 rounds x 3 minutes with a 30-second break between each round.
- Speed bag 2 rounds x 3 minutes with a 30-second break between each round.
- Skipping 10 minutes non-stop.
- Sit ups x 200.

Every Friday

- Strength Workout.
- Circuit Training non-stop.
- Resistant Band exercises.
- Squats jumping into air with Medicine Ball.
- Sprints 20 metre bursts x 6.
- Smash ball on the ground.
- Smash ball on the wall using torso by going side to side.
- Light dumbbells – explosive punching out at shoulder height.
- Smash truck tyres with ball.
- Belt harness around waist and pull weights, running fast for 20 metres.

SPARRING DAYS

Monday and Wednesday

- Depending on what stage in training camp, there was also Sparring on Saturdays.
- Wrap / Tape hands.
- Warm up / moving around / stretching 15 minutes non-stop.
- Shadow Boxing 3 rounds x 3 minutes with a 30-second break between each round.
- Sparring begins. Sparring – 6 rounds, progressively going to 8 rounds to 10 rounds x 3 minutes with a 30-second rest between each round.
- 2 weeks before the fight, 12 rounds of sparring would be done.
- Floor to ceiling bag 2 rounds x 3 minutes.
- Speed bag 2 rounds x 3 minutes.
- Skipping 10 minutes non-stop.
- Sit ups x 150.
- Dips x 25 of x 2 repetitions.
- Push ups x 25 x 2 repetitions.
- Stretching out for 10 minutes to finish workout.
- Massage once a week on a Saturday.

GARY

GARY JACOBS

'The Kid'

BIOGRAPHY

Gary Jacobs was born in Glasgow, Scotland in 1965.

After a short stint in Sydney, Australia with his family, Jacobs returned home to Scotland. He went to school and played soccer in the streets, and took up boxing at the age of fifteen, campaigning in twelve amateur contests.

Jacobs was also working and learning the ropes as a Goldsmith.

His Jewish father saw he had ability and a talent and after a training session in the local gym, he asked him if he would like to box, saying, "Do you fancy boxing?" Jacobs answered, "Not really!"

His Dad looked at him and said, "You'll get fifty pounds a fight".

Jacobs looked back and said, "Okay. Where are the gloves and when do I start?"

When I asked Jacobs what his reasoning was, he said, "If I was going to box, and train and spar and run, I was going to be paid for it. I loved the training, and I was working all week for fifty pounds, and I could make the same for one fight".

Jacobs turned professional in 1985, and two years later, he won the Scottish welterweight title. He then went on to beat the Commonwealth champion, Wilf Gentzler in Glasgow in 1988.

From there, like his fellow countryman, the 'Tartan Legend', Ken Buchanan, Jacobs would fight around the world in his opponents' backyards in tough fights. He moved to the 'big smoke' of London and signed with the shrewd promoter, Mike Barrett.

Barrett had promoted world champions, Charlie Magri, Alan Minter, and Jim Watt, and he secured a long-term deal with the London Albert Hall, and he had an allegiance of sorts with the other big boxing promoters, Mickey Duff, Jarvis Astaire, and Terry Lawless.

When you signed with Mike Barrett, there was no easy fights and this would definitely be the case with Jacobs, which suited him just fine. He wasn't driven by winning belts. Jacobs wanted to fight the best, get paid and go home. He trained hard with the mindset that if he was fitter and stronger than his opponent, he could out punch them and wear them down with his movement, and stamina and his strong southpaw jab and fast-darting left hand.

In his twenty fifth fight, he was matched with the unbeaten 35 wins and 0 losses, twenty-one-year-old English boxer, George Collins. Going into the fight, Collins had a 77 win / 1 loss amateur record, being beaten only once by Gary Stretch. He had the longest unbeaten record in Britain, and he was a tough proud boxer.

In the fight, Jacobs and Collins put on a great show, but Jacobs proved to be too strong and aggressive as the fight went on, measuring and connecting with his southpaw jab and hard left hands that made a dent in Collins chin. In the twelfth round, Jacobs hit Collins with a barrage of punches that forced him to take a knee but ended the fight on his feet.

It was a great performance from Jacobs that was made even more special to him as sitting ringside was the great English, Eastender, and Jewish world champion, Jack 'Kid' Berg.

In 1989, Jacobs had been matched to fight in New York in an eliminator for the WBA world title, with the winner fighting the 1984 Los Angeles Olympic Gold medallist Mark Breland.

After his original opponent pulling out late with an injury, Mike Barrett made a few phone calls and Jacobs signed up to fight the experienced scrapper from New York, Buddy McGirt.

McGirt had fought in forty-six fights, against tough competition in Meldrick Taylor, Howard Davis Jnr., and Saoul Mamby. Unbelievably, Barrett or Jacobs had never heard of him.

In the fight the experience was evident and McGirt was the better boxer, winning well on points.

Jacobs went home and three months later, he defended his commonwealth title, losing in Glasgow to the Canadian fighter, Donovan Boucher on points.

After a couple of good knockout wins Jacobs was matched to fight the hard as nails, big punching Londoner, Mickey Hughes in 1990.

It was such a huge domestic fight as there was a lot on the line for both boxers. Jacobs trained in America with trainer, Teddy Atlas and the 1984 Olympian, Hughes brought in John Conteh's old trainer, George Francis to try and give him the edge.

In the fight, Jacobs was so focused, boxing well and landing right uppercuts and hooks on the inside with Hughes reliant on looking for the big punch equaliser. Jacobs took some heavy punches but kept the pressure on. Jacobs suffered a cut to his left eye, but he was well ahead on points. In the seventh round, with Hughes both eyes damaged, he was punching his way back into the fight.

In the eighth round, Jacobs was pressing forward, ducking low, and about to throw a punch, and in a split second of a lapse of concentration, he dropped his right hand, leaving himself open, and Hughes threw a perfectly timed, powerful left hook that caught him flush, immediately sending Jacobs face-down onto the canvas at the York Hall. It was a tremendous battle.

Hughes fought on, losing to Donovan Boucher for his commonwealth title, and again to Lloyd Honeyghan. He retired in 1993.

Jacobs continued on and in 1992, he won the British welterweight title, to then pack his bags and challenge the French 26-win, 0 loss southpaw, Ludovic Proto in Paris, for the European title. Jacobs lost on a very bitter, controversial points decision.

Jacobs returned to the European champion's backyard four months later and gave the man from Guadeloupe a beating and a boxing lesson, doubling up on his jab, and out working the champion with left hooks to the body and head, wearing him down. In the ninth, Proto, battered, cut and bruised, was knocked down from a hard right hook and the fight was stopped. It was a brilliant performance from the Scotsman.

He returned home as the European welterweight champion going on a seven-fight winning streak that earned him a chance to fight one of the best fighters in the world, the southpaw defensive genius, Pernell Whitaker in 1995.

The fight was held in Atlantic City and Jacobs walked to the ring with the Star of David his shorts and the sound of bagpipes filling the air and his new promoter and cornerman, Mickey Duff, by his side. He was fighting for the WBC welterweight championship of the world.

Whitaker was an Olympic gold medallist in 1984, and he had won world titles in four different weight divisions and was considered as a pound-for-pound, all-time great.

In the fight, Jacobs took the fight to the champion, doubling up with his strong jab, and mauling his way inside with great success. Whitaker was very economical with his punches in the first six rounds, but he started to find his range from outside in the sixth round. Jacobs gave it everything and continued to pressure the man known as 'Sweet Pea'.

In the seventh, Whitaker boxed and moved around the ring, winning the round with the sharper punches. Whitaker was elusive and boxing well in the eighth, ducking and weaving until Jacobs came back with a great round nine, pushing Whitaker into the corner unleashing a strong attack. There was a shift in the fight with Whitaker boxing from the outside, but Jacobs never stopped pouring the pressure on. Jacobs fought an intelligent fight, winning the first half of the fight, until the champion fought his style of fighting from a distance in the second half.

With two rounds to go, Whitaker threw a wild hook that missed, and the momentum sent him off balance to the canvas while Jacobs was also trying to throw one of his own right hooks on the inside. The referee scored it a knockdown, setting the stage for a critical twelfth round. Jacobs needed a strong final round to have any chance of winning. Whitaker showed real urgency, punching strongly with his left hand. Jacobs was tired and arm weary. He had given everything in the fight. Whitaker poured it on, and the referee deducted a point from Jacobs. Whitaker smiled at the Scottish fighter, hitting him with a straight left hand that knocked him down. Jacobs could have stayed down but he got up quickly and Whitaker hit him with a right left combination that sent him down with seconds to go in the round. Jacobs got to his feet again and the bell rang to end the contest. Despite losing, Jacobs fought brilliantly, but in the end, Whitaker did what champions do and in the end he just found a way to win.

Whitaker fought on, fighting Jake Rodriguez, Wilfredo Rivera, Diobelys Hurtado, Oscar De La Hoya, and Felix Trinidad. He retired in 2001 after a fantastic Hall of Fame career.

Pernell Whitaker died in 2019 after being hit by a vehicle while crossing the road at Virginia Beach, Virginia.

Gary Jacobs fought on until 1997. He went from fighting for fifty pounds a fight, to fighting the best fighters in their backyards, with no easy paydays, or soft touches in a twelve-year career. When I talked to him, the last thing he said to me was, "If they were going to beat The Kid, they had to be good".

CAREER TOTALS

45 wins (26 KOs), 8 losses (2 KOs) and no draws.

GARY JACOBS – A DAY IN THE LIFE

What time did you get up in the morning?

7:00 am to do my roadwork. 6 days a week.

How far did you run?

5 miles every morning. Roadwork was very important for me and my style of fighting. I would do 4-minute miles consistently.

Did you stretch before you ran?

I would warm up and do some light stretching.

What did you do after your roadwork?

I would eat. Some toast with Philadelphia cheese and a cup of coffee and I drank water.

What did you do after breakfast?

I would watch a bit of TV and rest. Get ready for the gym.

How many days did you train in the gym?

5 days in the gym. I ran 6 mornings.

I would run for 18 minutes on a treadmill every Sunday.

what time did you go to the gym?

I would get to the gym at midday and train until 2:00 pm.

What was your favourite exercise in the gym?

Everything had to be done so I never had a favourite thing to do.

What did you eat for dinner?

I liked to eat pasta, and chicken in olive oil. I liked Peri water to drink.

What did you like to do for fun? I loved soccer. I enjoyed playing 5-a-side indoor soccer. I often played even when I was training for a fight. I also liked playing badminton.

Did you have a job?

Yes. I was a Goldsmith. I did jobs like setting jewels in rings, fixing peoples chains. I did this until I realised I could make more money boxing.

What time did you go to sleep?

10:00 pm.

5 days Workout in training camp

- Wrap hands.
- Warm up / Moving around / light stretching. Working on footwork – ring generalship – movement, slipping, bobbing, shadow boxing – 20 minutes non-stop.
- Shadow Box 10 minutes non-stop.
- Sparring begins – 6 hard rounds x 3 minutes with a 1-minute break in between each round. 5 days a week.
- 2 or 3 sparring partners, doing a total of 100 rounds in preparation for his opponent.
- 3 weeks sparring total. With 1 week to go until the fight, the strategy was to stay sharp, and peak when he was supposed to, doing daily shadow boxing and focus mitts.
- Jacobs trained to fight. He didn't train to lose weight.
- Circuit training to maximum output to be explosive.
- Sprints for 20 metres.
- Burpees x 30 x 2 repetitions.
- Push ups x 30 x 2 repetitions.
- Abdominal / Stomach exercises.
- Sit ups x 150.
- Leg Raises x 150.
- Jacobs did roadwork 6 days a week and he ran 18 minutes on a treadmill every Sunday.

GEORGE KAMBOSOS JR.

'Trial by Fire'

BIOGRAPHY

To be great you have to chase greatness. To be the best, you have to want it so badly that you are willing to do anything you can to be the best. You need to believe. You need to make sacrifices, and you need to live with the mentality that nothing will stop you. Nothing will ever come easy, and you need to go to hell and back to win and achieve greatness.

George Kambosos Jr. was born in June 1993, and after being bullied at school in Sydney, he started boxing at the age of eleven years old.

After boxing in 100 amateur bouts, Kambosos turned professional in 2013, fighting, and training, while struggling to live, working in a car salesman yard to pay the bills.

At the time, the sport of boxing in Australia was sporadic, with little media coverage, and even less big purses for their champions. World beaters like Sam Soliman, Sakio Bika, Michael Katsidis, Vic Darchinyan, Danny Green, Daniel Geale and Anthony Mundine were either thinking about retiring, actively fighting or chasing their next payday, which usually meant them travelling overseas.

Kambosos's father, was smart enough to realise this when he put the plan in place and put the question to his son, George. "I asked him how badly he wanted it, how badly he wanted to be a world champion. I asked him if he was willing to sacrifice everything to become world champion and George didn't hesitate. We had some money, but not much but we had a plan and George wanted to be a world champion so badly".

After 11 fights in the pros, the father and son team packed their bags and left Sydney and headed off to the Philippines to train in Manila, with the legendary, multi-weight world champion, Manny Pacquiao.

Kambosos would accompany Pacquiao on his hellacious roadwork runs around the hills of General Santos and through the years they spent together in training camps, Kambosos would enter into his own 'Trial by Fire' each time, enduring, learning and absorbing everything he could from the man known as the 'Pac-Man'.

Kambosos was on a road that only he could walk, fighting, struggling, training, sparring over 250 rounds with Pacquiao, while waiting for his chance, and in his mind. That was all he needed.

With tough hard-fought points wins against the Filipino Ray Perez in Vegas in January 2019, Mickey Bey in New York in December 2019, and a split decision win against the Sydney sun and enjoy the fruits of battle, but although beaten, he still had the fire in his belly to be a champion once more.

Devin Haney took on the challenge of Vasiliy Lomachenko in May 2023, beating the Ukrainian 'Matrix' in a very close, controversial decision in Las Vegas. Kambosos fought on, facing the English teak tough southpaw, Maxi Hughes for the IBO lightweight championship of the world. Again, everything was at stake for both fighters, as a loss to either could have been the end of the road, but a win would catapult them back into contention for a big money fight.

In the fight, Kambosos and Hughes fought hard, and they both fought with passion till the final bell, with the spartan warrior, winning a close majority decision in Shawnee, Oklahoma.

Maxi Hughes fought on, challenging the dangerous Mexican southpaw, William Zepeda, Segura in Las Vegas, in early 2023, where he retired in the fourth round.

Kambosos was a world champion again. He could have took a couple of easy fights, but instead he pushed to fight what he saw as the best lightweight in the world, Vasiliy Lomachenko.

After the Haney fight, Lomachenko was either going to retire or fight on, knowing inside he beat Haney. Could a man, a champion, a boxer like Lomachenko walk away from the sport he loved. For him, the answer was no.

Kambosos trained like an underdog, with memories of General Santos, the disappointments, the struggles and he sacrificed himself in the gym every day for sixteen weeks, running and sparring, with a burning fire inside.

Going into the fight, there was questions on whether Lomachenko was the same fighter, or had he had his one last great fight already, and would he grow old overnight. Lomachenko had *397 fights* in the amateurs with one loss. He fought often and he had been training hard as a young boy for many years, before he turned professional. There was a reasonable argument by many that Lomachenko stayed way too long in the amateurs and with all he achieved as a two time Olympic gold medallist, and his spectacular world championship achievements in the paid ranks, was Lomachenko tired of the sport, and was the brawler Kambosos getting the Ukrainian at the right time.

In the fight, Lomachenko fought brilliantly, focusing on Kambosos' mid-section, trying to take his legs, making him easier to hit. Kambosos fought with heart, throwing a two-fisted attack, but The Matrix counter-punched and anticipated his every move, hitting

Lee Selby in London in October 2020, Kambosos had proved he was a road warrior, a throwback fighter, a contender and a handful for anyone he faced.

After delay after delay, for Kambosos, it was announced that the Australian warrior would finally get his chance, and he would be fighting the talented unified champion Teofimo Lopez in New York in November 2021. Lopez had beaten Vasiliy Lomachenko on points in 2020 to become the best lightweight in the world. Going into the fight, Kambosos was a 13-win, 1-loss underdog.

After his dominant performance against Lomachenko, it was an easy assessment for the Las Vegas bookmakers. No one gave Kambosos a prayer. Kambosos and his father didn't need or want one. All they wanted was the chance.

In the fight, Kambosos came out aggressively, fighting fire with fire, and counterpunching Lopez trying to stamp his authority, never yielding, and never giving Lopez the chance to muster up any confidence or get into any kind of his New York groove.

Kambosos fought the fight of his life, taking big right hands from Lopez, and coming back with his own right hand knocking down the champion in the 1st round, and also being put down by a hard right hand in the 10th round to Raleigh strong with the belief inside of realising his dream of becoming the champion of the world. Going into the last two rounds, it was a close fight, and it was a case of who wanted to win it badly enough. In the end, it was Kambosos, that fought with heart and soul to win by a split decision to become the unified lightweight champion of the world. All the delays leading up to the fight, the family circumstances while in camp, the emotional drama and the years of struggling, all lead to the historic victory.

With little time to enjoy his win, it was announced that Kambosos would be facing the bigger, stronger boxer, Devin Haney (28 wins, 0 losses) in his first defence. The American was the WBC lightweight champion so everything was at stake as one would be the undisputed king of the lightweight division.

The fight was fought in Melbourne, Australia and in the fight, Haney used his strong jab to dictate the pace, the tempo and his jab set up his fast combination punching that took him to a unanimous points victory in June 2022.

Kambosos fought with heart, but he couldn't fight his fight. The two fighters met again in a rematch in the October and Haney technically outboxed Kambosos to make a statement as the best lightweight in the world.

Kambosos had been to the top and he had made enough money to go off and sail into

Kambosos with hard accurate shots, busting him up and breaking him down, physically and mentally. Lomachenko continued to throw spiteful hurtful left rips to Kambosos' body, catching him as he retreated, sending him down in the tenth round. The brave Kambosos stood up and Lomachenko went in for the finish, landing a flurry of hard punches to Kambosos' already broken body.

Kambosos was as graceful in defeat as he was ferocious in victory. He went on a journey, and he walked on a long hard road, never taking a backward step. He took a left when everyone was telling him to take a right. He chased greatness, and he realised his dream as a unified world champion against all the odds, and he fought with pride and courage every time he went into battle.

CAREER TOTALS

As of mid-2025, Kambosos Jnr's fight record is 22 wins (10 KOs) with 3 losses, no draws.

GEORGE KAMBOSOS – A DAY IN THE LIFE

What time to you get up in the morning?

6:30 am.

Do you do your roadwork in the morning?

Yes. I run from 7:15 am until 8:45 am every day.

How far do you run?

I run from 6 kilometres to 12 kilometres. I also do explosive sprint work once a week, which are 400-metre sprints, then jog, then 400-metre sprints. I also do leg strengthening on Mondays and Fridays.

Do you stretch out before you run?

Yes. Overall stretching. I also do resistance rubber band stretching which takes around 30 minutes.

What do you do after your running?

I do ab stomach exercises to strengthen my core. Sit ups, leg raises, side to sides. I then recover, rest, eat and sleep.

What do you have for breakfast?

Eggs, Oats, and I drink alkaline water (Alka power water). I eat high cards and protein in the morning.

What do you do after breakfast?

I rest. I take the kids to school if I'm in Sydney. I recover and I enjoy watching boxing on the TV. I have a light lunch and a couple of snacks.

What time do you go to the gym?

3:00 pm. I train until 6:30 pm. 6 days a week. Sunday is rest and family day.

What is your favourite exercise in the gym?

I like doing pad work. I go through shots, and I practice combinations, so they become second nature in the fight. I also like sparring, again so I can practice my punches.

What do you eat for dinner?

I eat high protein. Steak, fish, sweet potatoes, vegetables, pumpkin, and fruits and I drink water.

What do you do for fun?

I enjoy fishing. I like jet skiing, and I love fast cars. Supercar Audi R8. I'm also a family man.

What did you do for a job?

I worked in a car sales yard, and I also did a bit of personal training then I was a full-time boxer.

What time do you go to sleep?

I go to bed around 10:30 pm.

NON-SPARRING DAYS

- Wrap / tape hands.
- Warm up / Stretching whole body / Moving around 40 minutes non-stop.
- Skipping 6 x 3 minutes – 18 minutes non-stop.
- Shadow Box 6 rounds x 3 minutes with a 30-second break between each round.
- Focus mitts Depending on stage of training camp, 6–12 rounds x 3 minutes with a 30-second break between each round.
- Hit the Heavy Bag 3 rounds x 3 minutes with a 30-second break between each round.
- Remove Gloves.
- Warm Down exercises.
- Sit ups / crunches x 1000.
- Light weight dumbbells – Shadow boxing – moving around.
- Reaction / alertness / sharpness Drills to finish.

SPARRING DAYS

- Wrap / Tape hands.
- Warm up body / Stretch body / Moving around 40 minutes non-stop.
- Skipping 4 rounds x 3-minute rounds non-stop.
- Shadow Box 4 rounds x 3 minutes with a 30-second break between each round.
- Sparring begins. 2–3 Sparring partners waiting to spar. Depending on what stage in training camp, 6 to 12 rounds with a 30-second break between each round.
- Warm down body 40 minutes total to finish workout.
- Hit the heavy bag.
- Abdominal / Stomach exercises.
- Sit ups.
- Crunches.
- Leg raises.
- Hand Wraps off and have a drink and relax. Watch video of each sparring session with coach.

Kambosos would spar twice a week in training camp.

LESTER ELLIS

'The Master Blaster'

BIOGRAPHY

Lester Ellis was born in the Northern seaside town of Blackpool, England in 1965. He emigrated to Melbourne, Australia in 1968 with his parents and his two brothers with the chance and the hope of a better life down under. Not long after landing in their new home, Ellis' life was turned upside down, when his mother packed her bags and left one afternoon, without saying a word.

Life was unbelievably tough on Lester's father and brothers, and it hurt the young Ellis, hitting him harder than any punch he would receive in a fight. He struggled to accept that his mother wasn't coming home. He grew up quickly and was a tough street kid from the housing projects who was angry at the world. Not one for authority, Ellis wasn't one for school and he would 'wag' school and walk the streets, looking for ways to make money.

When I asked Lester about his life at school, he said, "I wagged school a lot, but I remember one time when I told my brother Keith that I needed a note to give to the teacher to explain why I was off. Keith told me he would take care of it for me."

Keith wrote the note and put the note in an envelope and sealed it, and handed it to me, telling me everything would be fine. I was happy and the next day, I handed the note in. The teacher read the note and looked at me and asked if my father had any problems. I was puzzled until the note was read out. As I stared on, the note was read out.

"Dear teacher. Lester couldn't come to school yesterday because he couldn't be fucked getting out of bed."

Ellis started boxing at twelve years old. His father worked as a meat worker by day, trying his best to raise his three sons and he also loved the sport of boxing, and he believed that the training and discipline would be beneficial in his sons' young lives.

Ellis would ride his bike for over an hour to get to the gym and he would always be the first one there and the last one to leave. He trained hard and channelled his anger in the gym and in the ring. Campaigning in fifty amateur fights, Ellis won four national championships and six state titles, to then turn professional on his eighteenth birthday.

He left school early and worked in the slaughterhouse, scraping the maggots off the cattle's hides that were hanging off the bloodied hooks.

In the gym, Ellis would train until he was exhausted and then fight through it and go for another three rounds of work. When I asked him about his training, he said, "I trained and fought angry. Hate gave me everything. Hate gave me the desire to win".

Turning professional, Ellis wasted no time, beating experienced tough fighters, Dennis Talbot (1974 Olympian), the Welsh champion, Steve Sims, and the Japanese champion, Kiyoshi Sasaki.

After only thirteen fights, Ellis challenged the Zambian, John Sichula for the Commonwealth super featherweight title in Melbourne. Sichula was unbeaten in eighteen fights, and he could punch.

Ellis took Sichula's best punches and although he was buzzed and hurt, he remained focused, and fought his way back into the fight, hurting the African to the body to win by a split decision and win the commonwealth title at age nineteen.

With little time to celebrate, Ellis was offered a shot at a world title in 1985, and he took it without hesitation. The champion was the South Korean southpaw warhorse, Hwan Kil Yuh. He was a tough, proud boxer who could box, punch and brawl.

In the weeks leading up to the fight, Ellis trained harder than ever before, living alone in a small caravan. He did his roadwork, and he ran four kilometres up a hill until he reached the top. He ran, he skipped, he shadow boxed, and he sparred. I asked him what he did in preparation for the biggest fight of his life, and he said, "All I did was sleep, rest, and I trained hard. I kept it simple. I would starve myself so I knew I would make the weight easy. I ran up 'Heartbreak Hill' every morning in twenty-four minutes. I was fit".

In the fight, Yuh lived up to his reputation as a tough, hard-headed champion, taking the fight to Ellis, landing some big punches to the teenager's head and body. Ellis fought hard, biting down on his gum shield, not allowing himself to take a backward step. Yuh was pressing but Ellis finished the fight stronger, out working the champion in the thirteenth, fourteenth and final round to win by a hard-fought split decision. Lester Ellis was the IBF Super Featherweight champion of the world at 19 years of age.

After the celebrations in the ring were over, he walked back to his dressing room. He was banged up. His kidneys were aching, and he was pissing blood. His nose was broken, and his face was torn. Instead of going to the hospital, Ellis pissed on a cloth and let the piss soak into his cuts then closed his ripped skin with butterfly tape and went home.

Hwan Kil Yuh returned to South Korea with his head held high, to then fight in one more contest, retiring at the end of 1985.

Years later, he was involved in a hit-and-run accident which left him in a vegetative state. He died in 2009.

With no time to stop and process what he had achieved, Ellis was back in the gym, almost immediately after his historic win, getting ready for his first defence of his world title.

His opponent was the experienced, teak tough Filipino, Rod Sequenan.

In the fight, the fifty-four fight southpaw brawler fought like a man possessed, desperate to win, and take the title back to the Philippines. It was a gruelling, exciting, battle of attrition that was fought on the inside. Ellis fought brilliantly, wearing the veteran puncher down, until he succumbed to Ellis's body punches followed by a barrage of punches in the thirteenth round.

Sequenan was battered and exhausted, but he fought hard, breaking the champions nose, and cheek bone, as well as cracking one of Ellis' teeth and leaving him with a scar over his eye that required fifteen stitches. It was a tremendous hard-fought victory.

Ellis had fought six times in his first year as a professional fighter. He fought eight fights in 1984, and as world champion he had been fighting in wars. After the Sequenan battle, and the injuries he sustained in the fight, he agreed to fight the English born fighter, Barry Michael in Melbourne. Going into the fight, Michael was twenty-nine years old, and he had fifty-five fights under his belt and he was moving down in weight to fight Ellis. He was a skilled boxer, and he was as hard as nails.

In the fight, Ellis was the bigger puncher, but Michael boxed well, and he was willing to take the big shots to land his own combinations. It was a tough, hard fight, and Ellis took a lot of punishment to his kidneys as well as a few low blows. Losing the weight didn't weaken Michael as the fight went on. He was strong at the weight and kept coming forward until the bell sounded to end the fifteen hellacious rounds.

Barry Michael won the contest by a unanimous points decision.

Michael went on to defend his world title four times, losing to the American Rocky Lockridge in 1987.

Ellis was devastated, but he was a fighter, and he fought on. He fought a rematch with John Sichula and the African beat him, stopping Ellis in the fourth round.

For Ellis, the loss was a loss, but his mind was still on losing his world title to Barry Michael.

Ellis could have left boxing, but he kept fighting. He went on an unbeaten thirteen-fight win streak, winning the light welterweight commonwealth title against the Jamaican born, Tony Laing, to then lose again in 1989 to Steve Larrimore.

Ellis and his brother Keith thought it was time for a change, so they decided to fight in America.

When I asked Ellis about the move, he said:

"We needed a change. If we were going to go it was now or never. The timing was right, and we were offered a few fights across there in Atlantic City and the money was good so why not. We did a bit of sparring, but we got caught in a hurricane over there and we had to get out of there, so we left and came home. We went back again but ended up in Puerto Rico. I had been offered a fight down there. When we finally got there, it was crazy. We drove into a compound with high walls around us. There were armed guards and pit bulls and lions and tigers in cages. It was like something you see on the TV. We looked around and the fighters who lived there were living in cells like they were in jail. The guy told us this was where we would sleep, and I told him to get fucked. We sorted that out and leading up to the fight, we would go to war in sparring. It was tough, hard sparring. They were like animals. I think they were testing me to see if I could handle it. As the fight got closer, we were told that the sixty thousand I was getting wasn't happening and they offered me ten thousand, then they said that I had to fight for free this one time, as no one knew me and the tickets weren't selling. We told them to get fucked and they weren't happy. We had to get out of there quickly. Keith saw a van and we jumped in and started it up. There were armed guards on the gate, but Keith put the foot down and crashed straight through the gate. It was crazy. We got to the airport and eventually we got out of there".

Ellis was at a turning point in his life. It was 1990. He signed with the shrew promoter, Bill 'Break Even' Mordey.

Mordey was behind Jeff Fenech and Jeff Harding in their careers as world champions, so it was an easy decision.

When I interviewed Lester at his home in Melbourne, I was curious to find out why Mordey wanted to sign him. When I asked him, he replied, "I don't know". He said I still had a lot left and he knew I was in a lot of hard fights, but he thought I could be a world champion again. Not long after I signed with him, he asked me to come up to Sydney to do a bit of sparring with Jeff Fenech. From memory, I was getting a couple of grand plus expenses, so I thought, "Why not?". I got to his gym and we both got ready. We went to work. Fenech was head butting me, so I told him to calm down a bit, but he didn't want to listen. I waited my time, and I hit him with a left rip to the liver and he went down like a bag of spuds. He was rolling about in pain. That was the end of the sparring. I was meant to go back the next day, but Mordey said the sparring was off. I was happy, I got paid and went home.

After knocking out the Brazilian, Luiz Carlos Dorea in two rounds, he was matched to fight the 44–1, Argentinian banger, Alberto Cortes.

In the fight, Ellis took an elbow to his eye, and he was struggling to see the punches coming. Cortes battered Ellis around the ring with the fight being stopped in the sixth round.

Lester Ellis continued to fight on, fighting in twelve contests, losing three. He won the IBO light welterweight world title in 1994, knocking out Al Coquilla in the first round, to then go on to win the IBO light middleweight championship of the world, beating Eric Alexander on points. He fought in a rematch in 1996 with the American, Calvin Grove, losing by knockout in the fourth round. It was now time to hang them up.

Ellis returned to the ring after six years to fight future WBA super middleweight champion, Anthony Mundine, losing by knockout in the third round.

Lester Ellis did everything the hard way. He fought in wars, getting busted up, and he body punched his way and fought his guts out, to win a world title as a nineteen-year-old boy.

He fought in a 49-fight career, with 41 wins that was filled with highs and lows, winning world titles in multiple weight divisions. He was a throwback fighter from yesteryear, who gave every bit of himself in the ring.

He was a fighter.

He was 'The Master Blaster.'

CAREER TOTALS

Ellis' fight record was 41 wins (28 KOs), 8 losses (5 KOs) and no draws.

"I HAD THE DEDICATION. I HAD SPEED AND POWER AND I GOT UP EVERY DAY TO RUN AND TRAIN TO BECOME A WORLD CHAMPION."

LESTER ELLIS

LESTER ELLIS – A DAY IN THE LIFE

What time did you get up in the morning?

I was up at 4:00 am.

Did you run in the morning?

I ran at 5:00 am every morning. I ran up this long hill. It was named 'Heartbreak Hill' and it was a killer. I ran up it in 23 minutes and it took me 15 minutes to get down again. I did this 3 times a week and I also ran 22 kilometres once every week. The other days, I ran 5 kilometres.

Did you stretch?

No.

What did you do after running?

I always did 500 sit ups on a concrete path. I also did 500 sit ups every night at the gym.

What did you eat for breakfast?

Porridge, low fat milk, and I had 2 salad sandwiches for my lunch every day. 6 weeks out from a fight, I would start to get the weight off and cut back on the food I ate.

What did you do after breakfast?

I liked to go for a walk then I would come home and have a rest. I would sleep from midday until 4:00 pm.

What time did you go to the gym?

I would drive to the gym and train, box or spar from 5:00 pm until 6:45 pm every day. 6 days. Sundays off.

What was your favourite exercise in the gym?

I loved to spar, and I loved doing sit ups. I did 1000 sit ups every day my whole career.

What did you eat for your dinner?

Fried Liver, sprouts, broccoli, vegetables and occasionally I would have fish.

Did you have a hobby?

I loved animals. I had white cockatoos, pigeons, rabbits, ferrets, and whippet dogs.

Did you have a job?

I used to fix people's push bikes. I worked in the slaughterhouse, shaving the maggots off the cows' hides.

What time did you go to bed?

I would sleep from midnight until 4:00 am.

NON-SPARRING DAYS

Tuesday and Thursday

- Skipping – hard and fast. 10 minutes non-stop, doing 3 revolutions (triples – most people do doubles when skipping)
- Sit ups x 500.
- Shadow Boxing 15 minutes non-stop at a fast ferocious pace.
- Neck strengthening exercises. Lying face down on the floor, hands behind back. Lift off and use the head and go on to your toes. Ellis would move his head forward and back taking the weight of his body. He would do this head movement 150 times non-stop.
- Ellis would use a 'Bullworker' and push the handles together and hold for 7 seconds. He would do this 30 times, twice a day.

SPARRING DAYS

- 6-week training camp.

Monday, Wednesday and Friday

- Wrap hands.
- Skipping 20 minutes fast non-stop.
- Sparring begins. 10 rounds x 3 minutes with a 1-minute break in between each round rounds.

Note: With 4 weeks away from the fight, Ellis would spar 10 rounds continuously, with no breaks in between rounds. 30 minutes non-stop.

- Ellis would Spar anyone and any size of a man.
- Sit ups x 500.
- Speed bag 10 minutes non-stop.
- Floor to ceiling bag 6 minutes non-stop to finish workout.
- Ellis would strip off and his brother would blast him with cold water from a hose.
- Saturday – Ellis would run 22 kilometres. Sunday off.

MICHAEL OLAJIDE JR.

'Smooth as Silk'

BIOGRAPHY

Michael Olajide Jnr. was born in Liverpool, England in 1963. Olajide's father was a former boxer, working in the tough Scouse shipyards until they became redundant and turbulent.

He moved to Vancouver, Canada for a better life, with his Nigerian family in 1970.

Olajide recalled, "I had a great family and special memories of my seven years in Liverpool."

The young thirteen-year-old Olajide started boxing when his father opened a small gym in East Vancouver, where he was put to work and pushed harder than the other boys in the gym.

His father recognised that his son had a special gift and while the softly spoken Olajide didn't look the part when he walked through the doors of the gym, as time passed, he surprised many with his tenacity, strength and skill as a boxer.

Olajide turned professional in December 1981, at eighteen years old, fighting and beating the experienced Al Ford on points in only his fourth fight. Ford had shared the ring with Ken Buchanan and Ray Mancini.

In 1985, the undefeated Olajide travelled to Suva, in Fiji to fight the veteran fighter, Sakaraia Ve, knocking him out in the ninth round to win the WAA middleweight title. I asked Olajide what made him go to Fiji, and he smiled, saying, "Why not? When I won, the money I made was enough to buy me a nice 67 Mustang."

Olajide continued, winning in impressive fashion, knocking out the tough Venezuelan fighter, Elio Diaz in seven rounds in 1985 to then fighting five times in 1986, becoming ranked as a top fifteen contender at middleweight.

Olajide and his father were now training out of Gleasons gym in Brooklyn and on any given day, there could be ten world champions working out there so Olajide was getting consistent world class sparring, taking his slick skills to another level. Olajide told me, "When I was training in Gleasons, the middleweight division was so strong. Anyone in the top ten could have been a world champion. It was always tough hard sparring and when you went to work, there was always quality fighters in Hector Camacho, Wilfred Benitez, Mustafa Hamsho, Vito Antuofermo, Chris Reid, and Donny Lalonde, all ready to go".

There would be fighters training there from all over the world and every one of them

wanted to be 'the man'.

In 1987, Olajide was 21–0, and he was matched to fight the dangerous fighter, Don Lee in Atlantic city. Lee had fought twenty-five fights and he had knocked out twenty-four of his opponents going into the fight.

Olajide out punched the puncher, knocking him down twice, stopping him in the ninth round.

This win earned him the chance to fight for the vacant IBF middleweight championship of the world. His opponent was the 1984 Los Angeles, Olympic gold medallists, and unbeaten fighter Frank Tate. Olajide was also unbeaten in twenty-three contests.

After fifteen hard fought rounds, Tate knocked down Olajide twice on his way to a unanimous points victory in Las Vegas. I asked Olajide what it felt like to train so hard and lose after fifteen hellacious rounds. Olajide again smiled, saying, "I had a lot going on in my life as a boxer. My relationship with my father was strained and I actually cut my hand a few weeks before the biggest fight of my life. The biggest thing was while no one knew, I had been seeing double vision for a while in sparring and in the ring and I kept it quiet so I could keep fighting and making money."

Olajide had been injured while sparring in Gleasons, twelve months earlier in 1986. It was a typical hard but routine sparring session with Olajide being caught by a wild uppercut that grazed his face and burst his lip, catching his right eye, blowing out the bottom tissue in a split second of a heated exchange of leather.

From that day onward, the unbeaten top contender saw life out of his right eye in a hazy double vision. No one picked it, not even the fight doctors, and Olajide or his father weren't telling them.

Frank Tate fought on, travelling to England to face Tony Sibson, knocking him out in the tenth round, to then lose his title to Michael Nunn in 1988.

Despite the loss, and his injury, Olajide fought on to face the tough and dangerous Iran Barkley in 1988.

In the fight, Olajide took the fight to Barkley, showing brilliant speed, boxing skill and power, knocking 'The Blade' down in the fourth round with a wild but perfectly placed left hook to then get knocked down by a big left hook to get up bravely and fight back until Barkley overwhelmed him with a barrage of punches in the fifth round.

The fight was stopped with Olajide on his feet, with the referee jumping in to prevent him from taking any more of Barkley's wild onslaught.

Barkley would go on to win the WBC middleweight championship of the world in his next fight in 1988, knocking out Tommy Hearns in the third round in Las Vegas. He fought on too long, fighting Tommy Hearns, Roberto Duran, Michael Nunn, Nigel Benn, James Toney, and Henry Maske.

Olajide fought on, grasping on to something that was gone, and it wasn't coming back. He was a slick, rhythm and reflex boxer, relying on split second adjustments and timing and losing the sight in one eye made it unfair and impossible to compete at any level in boxing, let alone fight in championship bouts.

In 1989, after a short winning streak, Olajide faced, the tough New York fighter from the Bronx, known as 'The Magician', Dennis Milton. Milton had been on a tremendous winning streak of his own, beating the dangerous knockout artist Gerald McClellan on points, and Robbie Sims and he also had an impressive amateur pedigree, beating Iran Barkley. Olajide was in fantastic shape physically albeit handicapped and compromised. Milton won the fight by a very tough, split decision. The loss for Olajide was the beginning of the end.

Milton fought on but was knocked out by Julian Jackson and losing to Bernard Hopkins, retiring from the sport in 1995.

Four months later, Michael Olajide, moved up in weight to fight Tommy Hearns in his 51st fight for his WBO super middleweight title in Atlantic City.

The Detroit Kronk Gym fighter had fought them all and had beaten James Kinchen in November 1988 to win the title and become the first boxer to win world titles in five different weight divisions.

Going into the fight with Olajide, Hearns had missed out on beating Sugar Ray Leonard, despite knocking down Leonard in the third and the eleventh round, going the distance with the super fight being declared as a draw in 1989.

For Olajide, this was it. All or nothing.

In the fight, Olajide walked out to 'Sweet Dreams' with Angelo Dundee in his corner and Hearns came to the ring with the song *Can't Touch This* blasting out, and Emanuel Steward behind him as always.

In the fight Hearns was stalking and cutting the ring off while Olajide was using his supreme fitness and smooth boxing skills, forcing the thirty-one-year-old to use his legs round after round. Hearns was relying on his jab, trying to set Olajide up with the one two, and Olajide was boxing and moving, hitting The Hitman with short sharp left hooks.

The tide turned when Hearns connected with a big right hand that knocked Olajide down in the ninth round. Never short on courage, Olajide got up quickly and came back, pushing an arm weary Hearns back towards the ropes, to finish the round strongly.

Hearns boxed from the outside the remainder of the fight, while Olajide knowing he needed a knockout to win, threw everything he had until the final bell rang. Hearns won by a unanimous decision at the 'Taj Mahal'.

Tommy Hearns fought on, fighting too long, chasing a greatness he already had, fighting in four decades, winning world titles in six different weight divisions.

Michael Olajide retired from boxing in 1991 at the age of twenty-seven.

The Silk was smooth, but beneath the good looks and the charisma, there was a toughness and resilience deep within, that got him through some very tough and challenging times and also fighting in an era of middleweight greats.

Michael Olajide's love for boxing has been with him all his life, still training his body and mind to perfection, as well as training and inspiring celebrities, top models and Hollywood actors in his studio gyms in New York and Los Angeles.

He is still smooth as silk.

CAREER TOTALS

Olajide Jnr's fight record was 27 wins 27 (19 KOs), 5 losses (2 KOs) and no draws.

What time did you get up in the morning?

5:00 am to run.

How far did you run?

I would run 5 miles every morning through reservoir, Central Park in New York City. I ran at a fast pace.

Did you stretch before you run?

No. Not much at all.

What did you do after your run?

I would do pull ups and push ups in the park.

What did you eat for breakfast?

I liked eggs and steak. Juice. I like natural foods.

What did you do after breakfast?

I relaxed. I usually had a nap around 10am before I went to the gym. I trained at the Gramercy Gym then I trained at Gleasons Gym.

What time did you go to the gym?

I would get to the gym for 5:00 pm and I would get ready to train or spar. I would train until 7:30 pm – 8:30 pm every night, 6 nights a week. You got great sparring there. Everywhere you looked, there was world champions and top 10 guys ready to spar.

What was your favourite exercise to do in the gym?

I did everything as it all had to be done, but I liked jumping rope, and I did a lot of shadow boxing. I practiced shadow boxing a lot.

What did you eat for your dinner?

I usually ate at 9:00 pm. I had steak, chicken, and pasta. I didn't eat much fish.

Did you have any interests or hobbies?

I like people and talking to people.
I like hanging out and talking. I loved the Oakland Raiders and the Richmond Packers, which was my local team.

Did you have a job?

No. I was a full-time boxer.

What time did you go to sleep?

10:30 pm.

NON-SPARRING DAYS

- Warm up / Calisthenics / Movement. Resistance training. 30 minutes total non-stop.
- Push ups.
- Burpees.
- Sit ups.
- Leg raises.
- Squats.
- Jumping Jacks.
- Shadow Boxing 4 rounds x 3 minutes with a 1-minute break between rounds. This was very important in his training as he practiced his combination punching and technique.
- Hit the Heavy Bag 7–10 rounds x 3 minutes with a 1-minute break between each round.
- Focus Mitts was every alternate day.
- Jump Rope 30 minutes non-stop.
- Speed Bag 3 rounds x 3 minutes.
- Double End Bag (Jab Bag) 3 rounds x 3 minutes.
- Pull ups / Chin ups. Using his fingertips to pull himself up to exhaustion.

SPARRING DAY

Alternate Days

- Wrap hands.
- Warm up / Calisthenics / Moving. 20 minutes.
- Push ups.
- Burpees.
- Sit ups.
- Leg raises.
- Squats.
- Jumping jacks.
- Shadow Box 4 rounds x 3 minutes with a 1-minute break.
- Sparring would begin. There was always sparring going on in the gym. Mustafa Hamsho, Donny Lalonde, Chris Reid, and Vito Antuofermo were always there, ready to go.
- Sparring 10–15 hard rounds x 3 minutes with a 1-minute break between each round.
- Mitt work x 6 rounds on alternate days.
- Jump Rope 30 minutes non-stop.
- Speed Bag 2 rounds x 3 minutes non-stop.
- Double End Bag 2 rounds x 3 minutes non-stop.
- Pull up / Chin ups using fingertips until exhaustion.

VASSILIY JIROV

'The Tiger of Kazakhstan'

BIOGRAPHY

Vassiliy Jirov was born in 1974 in the industrial town of Balqash, Kazakhstan. Jirov was born into hardship that made him resilient tough and hungry.

With a limited education program, Jirov excelled in wrestling before turning to boxing at eleven years old.

In 1996, after ten years of sacrifice, commitment and also an extreme regime of physical and mental training which included being taken out on a huge surrounding lake by boat and being told to jump in the freezing water and swim back to shore. Jirov would have to swim for three hours to get back to dry land. Other unconventional methods had the young Jirov, and his gym team mates, running the gauntlet, running as fast as they could, along a long corridor with the objective being to get to the safety of the open door at the end and slamming the door shut while being chased by a ferocious dog. Jirov was given a piece of short thick rope to ram into the dog's open jaws to try and lessen the attack while fighting off the crazed canine. There were also less extreme methods of running in thick snow in sub-zero temperatures and training until the body could take no more.

In 1996, Jirov represented Kazakhstan at the Atlanta Olympic games, winning the Gold medal and also the Val Barker trophy for being the most outstanding boxer of the tournament.

Jirov turned professional after the Summer games leaving the amateurs with a tremendous 217 fights with only 10 defeats.

He moved to America and made his debut in early 1997, winning by knockout in Las Vegas.

Jirov feared no one, racking up a 20-wins-with-no-losses record to get his chance to fight for the IBF cruiserweight championship of the world. His opponent was 'King' Arthur Williams.

In the fight, Jirov was like an animal, stalking and attacking Williams, going to the body with hard thudding shots, breaking him down, eventually hurting him with a single punch to the mid-section that forced Williams to take a knee, to then rise to his feet to be hammered by Jirov in the seventh round.

After all the years of training and fighting and the years of struggling in Kazakhstan, Vassiliy Jirov realised his dream of becoming the cruiserweight champion of the world.

There was a lot of talk about Roy Jones Jnr. moving up to fight Jirov but in the end, it was just talk. Jirov was unbeaten in five years with thirty-one fights and twenty-seven stoppages. He was a beast.

After losing fourteen months due to contractual issues, it was now 2003.

Jirov returned to face the two-weight champion, James Toney. A tough hard fight but Jirov trained hard to be ready for the man known as 'Lights Out'.

In the fight, Jirov was the aggressor, forcing Toney backwards to the ropes and banging his body with hard punches. Toney absorbed the punches and seemed happy on the ropes, countering and fighting tough, making it a shootout slugfest. Jirov kept stalking and he was firing off big shots from his southpaw stance, making Toney cover up with his brilliant shoulder roll defence that had served him so well since 1988. Toney boxed without wasting any of his punches, while Jirov pressed and pressured, and he was relentless and throwing everything he had. Going into the twelfth round, it was a battle of attrition, a close fight with both champions going to war, exchanging big punches and both hurt and exhausted. Toney caught Jirov with an accumulation of single hard hooks that took their toll on the tough champion, and he went down with twenty seconds to go in the fight.

Jirov rose up to his feet and the bell rang to end one of the greatest cruiserweight battles ever. Going into the twelfth round, I had Jirov winning the fight. At the end, I scored it a draw. The judges saw things much differently, with 117–109 117–109 and 116–110 all for James Toney. Jirov was never given a rematch.

Toney kept fighting until 2017, moving up to heavyweight, and ending his career with 77 wins, 10 losses and 3 draws.

Vassiliy Jirov carried on fighting until 2009, moving up to heavyweight.

CAREER TOTALS

The Tiger of Kazakhstan retired after a 42-fight career with 38 wins (32 KOs), 3 losses (1 KO) and one draw.

VASSILIY JIROV – A DAY IN THE LIFE

What time did you get up in the morning?

I got up at 6:00 am to do my roadwork.

How far did you run?

I did different things when I ran. I would walk, then run. I would run for 1 hour. I would do jogging then sprinting hard, then jog again until I was tired. This was interval training.

Did you stretch your body before running?

Yes. Maybe 15 minutes. I focused on my mind before I run.

What did you do after roadwork?

I would shadow box, and I did some weights. I would also swim on non-sparring days.

What did you eat for breakfast?

Cereal, eggs, green vegetables, fresh orange juice. Fresh vegetables and fruit.

What did you do after breakfast?

I would read. Learning kept my mind sharp.

How many days did you go to the gym?

My first training was 6:00 am running. My second training was weights at 9:30 am. My third training was at 4:00 pm, sometimes 5:00 pm. I trained 7 days a week.

What time did you finish in the gym?

I trained 3 times a day which was around 7 hours every day. I focused my mind, and I trained hard to push myself to create possibilities.

What did you eat for dinner?

Salads, nuts, light protein, vegetables and fruits. I drank water.

What did you do for fun, or did you have a hobby?

I liked reading books and I enjoyed making and crafting wood.

Did you have a job?

Yes. I was a welder. I finished school diploma, and I was boxer.

What time did you go to bed?

I always tried to go to sleep when the sun goes down. No later than 8:00 pm.

NON-SPARRING DAYS

- 9:30 am – swimming then rest.
- Stretching / Moving around 20 minutes.
- Jump rope 10 minutes non-stop.
- Wrap Hands and prepare mind and body.
- Heavy Bag 10 to 12 rounds x 3 minutes with a 1-minute break.
- Stretching 5 minutes.
- Speed work – Sprints 20 metres interval training. Sprint, jog, run, sprint. 20 minutes non-stop.
- Speed Bag 6 minutes.
- Double End Bag 6 minutes.
- Stretching out body for 15 minutes.
- Rest and analyse what has been done.

SPARRING DAYS

3 or 4 days a week

- Wrap Hands.
- (Look around and create things in your mind – focus on what the sparring will be.)
- Stretching out / moving around 20 minutes non-stop.
- Jump Rope 10 minutes non-stop.
- (Walk around mind focused)
- Shadow boxing 5 minutes.
- Sparring begins – There is always 3 or 4 or 5 sparring partners waiting.
- Depending on training camp, Sparring is 6 rounds x 3 minutes with a 1-minute break in between each round rounds.
- As camp progresses, Sparring goes to 10 rounds then 12 rounds x 3 minutes.
- Stretching out 5 minutes.
- Speed Bag 2 rounds x 3 minutes.
- Think about the sparring / talk to coach what can be done better.

VIC TOWEEL

'The Benoni Buzzsaw'

BIOGRAPHY

Vic Toweel was born in Benoni, Gauteng, in South Africa in 1928. He started boxing as a young boy, training with his father who had built a gym which was a corrugated iron shed at the back of their house. It was rough and ready, but it was all they needed. Toweel would train hard with the iron sheets of the shack heating up under the African sun, making it like an oven inside.

Toweel fought in 190 amateur contests with 188 wins, and he represented South Africa in the 1948 Olympic Games in London.

He turned professional in 1949.

Working as a wood carver and a salesman in Benoni, relying heavily on purses from fighting, Toweel trained and worked hard with the belief and the dream of becoming a world champion.

In only his eleventh fight, he fought the English boxer, Stan Rowan, beating him on points to win the Commonwealth and British Empire Bantamweight champion.

In May 1950 Toweel, fighting in only his fourteenth fight as a professional, challenged the legendary champion, Manuel Ortiz for the Undisputed Bantamweight Championship of the world.

The American had won the world Bantamweight Championship in 1942, beating Lou Salica on points and he defended his title fifteen times, to then lose to Harold Dade in 1947. Ortiz beat Dade, two months later in their rematch to regain his title. After defending his title with pride, dignity and honour, he would travel to Johannesburg South Africa to fight the twenty-one-year-old 'Benoni Buzzaw'.

In the fight, Toweel fought brilliantly, fighting, and boxing the experienced champion over fifteen rounds, beating him to become the undisputed Bantamweight champion of the world. Vic Toweel was South Africa's first and only undisputed world champion.

Manuel Ortiz fought on until 1955, ending a seventeen-year career as an all-time great with a reported one hundred and thirty fights including twenty-nine losses and three draws.

Toweel fought a further three times that year, knocking down Englishman Danny O'Sullivan fourteen times, before the referee stepped in to halt proceedings in the tenth round. He fought five times in 1951, finishing the year with a great points win over the former European champion, Luis Romero to then start 1952 with another impressive win on points over the European champion from Glasgow, Scotland, Peter Keenan at the Rand Stadium in Johannesburg.

Toweel fought Georges Mousse three times, beating the Frenchman on points twice and one contest was scored as a draw.

After these bouts Toweel began having trouble with his eyesight, seeing double vision. He was also struggling to boil down to make bantamweight, and something had to give.

In November 1952, Toweel took on the challenge from the tough and relentless Australian, Jimmy Carruthers.

Carruthers was a fellow 1948 Olympian and an unbeaten Australian champion.

In the lead up, the fight with Toweel was postponed for six months due to Carruthers suffering a blood infection which almost resulted in him having his foot cut off.

He recovered well and in the fight, with 28,000 fans cheering, the Australian, Carruthers charged at Toweel, showing unbelievable hand speed that never gave the champion a chance to breathe, let alone fight, throwing over one hundred and ten punches in an onslaught that ended at 2:19 seconds of the first round, giving the fight clearly to Carruthers.

The two champions fought again four months later in a tremendous battle of attrition, with Carruthers knocking out Toweel in the tenth round.

Toweel fought on, moving up to featherweight and retiring in 1954 with a record of 32 fights with 3 losses and 1 draw.

He was the undisputed bantamweight champion when there was only eight championship weight categories, and Vic Toweel was one of the eight champions of the world.

1928–2008.

CAREER TOTALS

Toweel finished his career with 28 wins (14 KOs), 3 losses (2 KOs) and 1 draw.

VIC TOWEEL – A DAY IN THE LIFE

What time did you get up in the morning?

5:30 am every day to run.

How far did you run?

I ran for 1 hour. I would also do 200 metre drills. I would run backwards for 200. I would sprint for 100 metres then jog for 200 metres then sprint for 100 metres and then run backwards until I was exhausted.

Did you stretch before you ran?

Yes. Before and after.

What did you do after running?

I stretched out and I did push ups and sit ups, alternating for 25 minutes total.

What did you have for breakfast?

Poached eggs, water, orange juice. If I was making weight, I would skip breakfast.

What did you do after breakfast?

Rest and relax.

What time did you go to the gym?

4:00 pm until 6:00 pm every day. 6 days a week. Sunday off.

What did you eat for dinner?

Grilled meats and salad. Water.

what did you do for fun?

I loved to dance. Jiving. I loved music.

what job did you do?

I was a full-time boxer. I relied on purses from fighting. Life after boxing, I was a travelling salesman on the road.

What time did you go to bed?

8:30 pm every night.

NON-SPARRING DAYS

- Stretching full body 20 minutes.
- Warm up / moving around / Shadow Boxing 3 rounds x 3 minutes with 30-second breaks in between.
- Heavy Bag 4–6 rounds x 3 minutes with a 30-second break in between each round.
- Floor to ceiling / Double End Bag 4 rounds x 3 minutes.
- Speed Bag 4 rounds x 3 minutes.
- Skipping 15 minutes non-stop.
- Floor exercises – 25 minutes.
- Sit ups.
- Chin ups.
- Push ups.
- Neck exercises (pushing hard on head using palm of the hand to press and push against the palm of hand. Alternate to do each side of neck.
- Pushing the fist upwards while pressing down with hand to create pressure. Also press fist downwards while pushing upwards to create resistance.

SPARRING DAYS

- Stretching full body 20 minutes.
- Warm up / Moving around/ Shadow Boxing 3 rounds x 3 minutes with 30-second breaks in between.
- Sparring begins – 3 Sparring partners waiting.
- Depending on training, 6 rounds x 3 minutes with 30-second breaks in between.
- Training progresses from 6 rounds up to 15 rounds of hard sparring with 30-second breaks in between each round.
- Skipping 15 minutes non-stop.

AZUMAH NELSON

'Zoom Zoom', 'The Accra Warrior'

BIOGRAPHY

Azumah Nelson was born in 1958. As a young boy, he would hustle around the dirt streets of the old port of Accra, selling glass bottles for money and also climbing trees, gathering and cutting the husks off coconuts to sell them for money to eat.

Nelson would grow strong, working in a quarry from dawn till dusk, breaking stones with a hammer. He started boxing in the streets when he was nine years old, and soon after, he found *The Akotoku Academy* to train and practice boxing. Nelson would do whatever he could to get some money to eat then he would practice boxing at the gym every day, and on Sundays, the training would stop, and the young boxers would sit on the ground and watch old film from America of Joe Louis and Jersey Joe Walcott.

Nelson had fifty-two fights with only two defeats as an amateur and he became part of the Ghana national boxing team, known as 'The Black Bombers'. He won the gold medal in the 1978 Edmonton Commonwealth Games at the age of twenty-one. Nelson turned professional in June 1979, fighting and winning a ten-round fight on his debut in the December of that year.

It was now 1982, and after thirteen fights, and two and a half years since turning professional, Azumah Nelson was offered the chance to fight for a world title. Promoter, Don King was looking to fill a gap with only weeks to go and he needed to find someone who would be a test for his golden goose, the WBC Featherweight champion of the world, Salvador Sanchez. The fight was to be a night that would showcase the talented Sanchez, and his formidable skills and Nelson was brought in purely as a dance partner.

In the fight, the young, unknown African fought hard until his arms and legs could do no more, but the supreme engine of Sanchez was too much, knocking Nelson down in the fifteenth round at Madison Square Garden.

A few weeks later, tragedy struck when Salvador Sanchez was killed in a car crash on a country road, while trying to pass a tractor and trailer near his hometown of Santiago. He was twenty-three years old.

Nelson kept training and winning, fighting four times in 1983 while waiting for his chance and in 1984 he was matched to fight the tremendous puncher from Puerto Rico, Wilfredo Gomez.

Gomez had just beaten Juan Laporte on points to win the WBC Featherweight title and with only one defeat in his ten-year career at the hands of Salvador Sanchez, Gomez was a dangerous powerful puncher, with 32 knockout wins in a row, earning him the nickname of 'Bazooka'.

Nelson trained for three months in the heat and humidity of Ghana before moving to the cold and wet of Ohio for three months to be ready for the might of Gomez. Going into the fight Nelson was confident as he knew he could punch, racking up fifteen knockouts in eighteen fights.

In the fight, Nelson was relentless with aggressive pressure, going to the body and head of the champion. Gomez fought back, landing big right hands but the combination onslaught from Nelson was breaking Gomez down. Nelson was catching Gomez with solid right hands and uppercuts, rocking him, and leaving him struggling to stay upright. Gomez was brave and he fought back but after a right hook, left hook combination in the eleventh round, Gomez's legs gave way, and it was over.

Azumah Nelson had beaten their champion and broke the hearts of the people of Puerto Rico, but thousands of miles away, there was celebrations and singing and dancing in the streets of Ghana, where they rejoiced in unison for their champion of the world.

From that day on Azumah Nelson travelled to foreign lands, banging the drum for himself and his people, fighting in tough bruising fights against Marcos Villasana, and Mario Martinez, going to England and battering the elusive Pat Cowdell with a huge left hook come uppercut that nailed him to the canvas in the first round. He then returned to face the brave Boxer, Jim McDonnell at London's Royal Albert Hall where he pummelled the Englishman with thudding jabs, and hard left hooks, knocking him down four times until the referee waved it off in the twelfth round.

In 1990, Nelson relinquished his super featherweight title to move up to lightweight to challenge the brilliant defensive southpaw boxer Pernell Whitaker for his WBC and IBF titles in Las Vegas. Not only was this going to be Nelson's biggest and toughest fight of his eleven-year career, but unbeknownst to many, Nelson had been going through heartbreaking personal struggles as his wife had been battling cancer for the last couple of years and her health was deteriorating when he left to go into training camp in Ohio.

In the fight, Azumah Nelson was a million miles away. He was there but his heart was back in Ghana with his wife. He was punching but walking into Whitaker's fast hand flurries, while feeling nothing. Whitaker threw 578 jabs and landed 286, and Nelson found the target with 179 punches. Nelson took the loss and went home to be with wife. Not long after arriving home, Nelson's wife passed away.

Azumah Nelson was grieving but fought on and next up was the fast experienced boxer Juan Laporte. The Puerto Rican had shared the ring with Salvador Sanchez, Rocky Lockridge, Eusebio Pedrosa, Wilfredo Gomez, Barry McGuigan, Julio Cesar Chavez, Lupe Suarez, and John Molina and he had seen it all.

The fight was held in Sydney Australia and the winner would face the 'Thunder from Down Under' Jeff Fenech. The fight was a close affair with both champions having success but in the end, Nelson's jab was the deciding factor, winning on points. Juan Laporte fought on, but he was never the same, losing to Hector Lopez and Kostya Tszyu.

The road warrior, Nelson returned to Las Vegas eight months later to fight the unbeaten three weight world champion, Jeff Fenech for the WBC super featherweight title. Fenech was making his debut on American soil and not only did he want to have Nelson's scalp, he wanted his fourth title in another weight division, chasing fame and fortune and greatness in the home of the brave.

The fight was held outdoors at the Mirage and when the two fighters stepped into the ring it was ninety-two degrees Fahrenheit (33 Celsius). Fenech, at twenty-seven, and Nelson at thirty-two, both looked in fantastic shape and both fighters set a tremendous frenetic pace, going toe to toe, with flurries from Fenech, to hard thudding punches from Nelson, with the majority of the fight being fought in the neutral corner. Nelson was the better boxer, with better skills and better quality of punches. Fenech was all out brawling, throwing flurries, showing little defence but being the aggressor, cutting the ring off and landing eye catching punches in close fought rounds. It was a great fight that went to the score cards, ending in a draw.

A lot has been said about the fight. I watched the fight in 1991, and I also scored it a draw. Since then, I've watched it many times and I still scored it a draw. I gave Nelson the 1st, 2nd, 4th, 6th, 8th, 9th, and I gave Fenech the rest of the rounds and I gave Fenech the third round even though Nelson hurt him, making his legs buckle, and I gave Fenech the last round.

With controversy comes frustration and anger so the rematch was signed, with the fight being staged in Melbourne.

It was the biggest fight in Australia since Jack Johnson fought Tommy Burns for the heavyweight championship of the world in 1908. Expectations were high for Fenech to not just beat Nelson, but to outbox, out work and break him down to then knock the thirty-three-year-old African out in devastating fashion in front of his adoring fans.

Fenech promising to send Nelson back to Ghana in a body bag. Nelson prepared in Spain, and Fenech in Sydney. I remember the fight like it was yesterday. I thought Nelson would beat Fenech and I flew down from Sydney with great excitement and expectations for a great event.

Nelson was fighting in his seventeenth world championship fight, and he was a proud world champion for eight years. With singing and drums and cowbells banging in wild jungle beats, and chants of "Asem be re ba ooo." To this day I don't know what it means, but it was unforgettable and magic.

Nelson's entourage dressed in the colours of Ghana danced their way to the edge of the ring. A stone faced Fenech walked out with his head down with his cornermen, looking to do a number on the man they called 'Zoom Zoom'.

In the fight, Nelson hit Fenech with a big right hand that shook him to his boots in the first round. Fenech fought back in the second round, but Nelson was faster and stronger and was not only out-working the Australian, but he was also out-classing him. Nelson was setting traps and showing effective aggression that Fenech had no answer for, and in the eighth round, he fell into his trap, and leaving himself wide open, Nelson landed with his famed left hook and a two-punch flurry, finishing Fenech off with a right hand that relieved him of his senses, and his legs gave in. Fenech collapsed to the canvas and somehow he got up to then be drilled by six unanswered punches to end proceedings. It was a tremendously convincing performance which left no doubt that Nelson was the superior fighter at that weight. Jeff Fenech fought on until 1996, but the spark had gone.

After giving the American boxer, Calvin Grove something to think about, while giving him a controlled, drawn-out beating, Nelson took on yet another challenge, travelling to Mexico City to face Gabriel Ruelas at the Estadio Azteca.

On the night, there was a recorded one hundred and thirty-four thousand Mexican fans packed inside with many thousands outside the stadium trying to hustle their way in to watch their hero Julio Cesar Chavez systematically breakdown Greg Haugen in the fifth round. The crowd were ravenous after watching Ruelas take on Nelson, losing on points in a tough competitive fight. Nelson fought a strong controlled fight with the much younger Ruelas giving all he had, particularly in the eighth round but Nelson came back, unfazed by the Mexican, to finish strongly in the final rounds to win on points. Ruelas was angry and disputed the judges scoring, and Nelson smiled and said quietly "I was the professor, and he was the student".

Azumah Nelson fought on, facing 'Jesse' James Leija in four fights which took place over the last years of his long career. It was a great trilogy of fights with Leija fighting in a close decision draw, to then beat Nelson on points, and then be knocked out by Nelson. Leija went on to defend and lose his title against Ruelas. Nelson challenged Gabriel Ruelas in a rematch but this time he pummelled the Mexican with left hooks until he succumbed in the fifth round, leaving the referee to stop him from further punishment, and snatching his title away in a spiteful, emphatic victory.

It was now 1997 and Azumah had been fighting for seventeen years, fighting in forty-three fights and many championship battles along the way.

There had been fighters before him that came out of Ghana, like, Roy Ankrah, Floyd Robertson, David 'DK Poison' Kotei, (Ghana's first world champion) and Osumana Akaba, but none had captured the hearts of the people like Azumah Nelson.

He could have walked away but he fought on, defending his title against the experienced 'Artful Dodger', former WBA super featherweight champion Genaro 'Chicanito' Hernández.

The Mexican was a durable fighter, and he was always hard to hit, dodging and slipping out of harm's way, and he was a tremendous boxer, and he was hungry for victory over Nelson.

In the fight, Nelson was counter punched by Hernández, using his long reach to out box him. Nelson was aggressive and fighting angry due to frustration from not being able to land on the elusive Mexicans chin. Nelson knew he had to get inside and work Hernández's body. At the end of the seventh round as the bell rang, Nelson was in full flight, and he landed with two left hooks that found the target. Hernández was as hard as they come having fought through tough battles all his life, most notably going into a fight with Oscar De La Hoya with a badly broken nose.

The Mexican dropped and he instantly spat out his gum shield and held his throat in distress. The referee and the officials at ringside gave Chicanito five minutes to recover as it was agreed that the left hook was thrown after the bell. Having been hit by a non-intentional punch, Hernández he could have milked it, but didn't. It was *not* Genaro Hernández's style. Hernández could have sat on his stool and won the world title, but Hernández fought on. Round eight continued and he used every bit of experience he had, doing what he could to win the rounds, slipping and spoiling Nelson's chances of landing the knockout punch he needed. All things considered, it was a great performance and the Mexican deserved to win.

Genaro Hernández defended his title on three occasions. He took on the challenge of a young Pretty Boy Floyd Mayweather in 1998, which was to be his last time in the ring. Mayweather was too fast, too accurate, and too much, winning in eight rounds.

Genaro Chicanito Hernández retired in 1998, and passed away in June 2011, after years of fighting a rare cancer. He was forty-five years old. Floyd Mayweather paid for his funeral.

After the loss to Hernández, Nelson returned home. He could enjoy himself and finally relax. He could eat whatever he liked. He could eat Fufu, Jollof rice, and Chinese take away. Life was good.

Nelson was thirty-nine years old and happily retired but thousands of miles away, a plan had been laid out by Top Rank boxing to entice him to lace them up one more time. His opponent was Jesse James Leija. The logic was they had fought three times with one victory a piece and one draw so the fourth fight would be the decider. Nelson bought the logic, and the fight was signed for the summer of 1998, so once again Nelson returned to Leija's hometown of San Antonio to fight at The Alamodome.

In the fight Leija boxed well, flicking the jab out and Nelson kept coming forward hoping to land his armed and dangerous left hook so he could get paid and go home. Leija continued to box with Nelson stalking and landing effective punches to the body but after twelve rounds, the decision went to Leija. For Nelson it was over. He returned home, the people's champion.

Jessie James Leija fought on, facing Shane Mosley, Ivan Robinson, Hector Camacho Jnr., Micky Ward, Kostya Tszyu, and Arturo Gatti. He retired in 2005.

Azumah Nelson left boxing a happy man. He had nothing else to prove. He gave the people of Ghana and the people of the African nations, something to believe in and something to be happy about every time he fought.

Many have followed in his footsteps. Nana Yaw Konadu, Ike Quartey, Joshua Clottey, Joseph Agbeko, Manyo Plange, Richard Commey, and Issac Dogboe and while they have all represented Accra and Ghana with pride and passion, there will never be another Zoom Zoom.

CAREER TOTALS

Nelson's fight record was 38 wins (27 KOs) 6 losses, (1 KO) and 2 draws.

What time did you get up in the morning?

5:30 am.

Did you do your roadwork in the morning?

Yes. I wrapped my hands, and I would run for 1 hour and a half.

Did you stretch before you run?

Small stretching and I shadow boxed to warm up. I finished training around 8:30 am.

What did you do after your run?

I would run to the gym and hit the heavy bag for 1 hour. I would take a bath and have some hot tea. I relaxed then I ate.

What did you eat for breakfast?

I had hot tea and sardines, and I had fruit and water. I would then relax and rest until it was time to train again.

What time did you go to the gym?

I would go at midday until 1:30 pm then I would go back again at 5:00 pm until 7:30 pm.

What was your favourite exercise to do in the gym?

I liked everything. I had to do everything. I trained three times a day with Sunday off.

What did you eat for dinner?

I had rice, meats and salads and vegetables and I had water and fresh juice.

What did you do for fun?

I love the movies. I love cowboy films.

Did you have a job?

I sold crabs around the houses. I cut down the coconuts and sell them. I also had a job breaking rocks with a hammer in a quarry. I would do this and train. It made me tough.

What time did you go to bed?

10:30 pm.

NON-SPARRING DAYS

- Every morning after running – Hit the Heavy Bag for 1 hour.
- Go to the gym every day at Midday.
- Warm up / Light stretching / Moving around 20 minutes non-stop.
- Skipping 15 minutes non-stop.
- Heavy Bag 6 rounds x 3 minutes with a 1-minute rest in between.
- Floor exercises for 20 minutes.
- Sit ups.
- Crunches.
- Push ups.
- Shadow Boxing 3 rounds x 3 minutes non-stop.
- Go back to the gym at 5:00 pm.
- Warm up / Stretching / Moving / Wrap hands. 20 minutes total.
- Shadow Boxing 3 rounds x 3 minutes with a 1-minute break in between each round rounds.
- Heavy Bag 15–20 rounds x 3 minutes with a 1-minute break in between each round.
- Skipping 15 minutes non-stop.
- Shadow Box 2 rounds x 3 minutes to finish workout.

SPARRING DAYS

- Every morning after running – Hit the heavy bag for 1 hour.
- Midday. Every day. Go to the gym and exercise then go home to rest.
- 4:00 pm – Nelson would chop trees for 20 minutes before he Sparred. He wanted to push himself and go in feeling the fatigue from wood chopping as he felt it helped him in his fights. He would have his hands wrapped before.
- 5:00 pm sparring session.
- Warm up / Stretching / Moving around 15 minutes total.
- Sparring begins.
- Sparring 15–20 rounds x 3 minutes with a 1-minute break in between each round.
- Skipping 15 minutes non-stop.
- Shadow Boxing 2 rounds x 3 minutes to finish workout.

CARLOS PALOMINO

'King'

BIOGRAPHY

Carlos Palomino was born in San Luis, Sonora, Mexico in 1949. After years of struggling to make ends meet, Palomino's mother and father decided to cross the border to Los Angeles with the hope of a better life for their young family. While waiting for their visa, the eight-year-old Palomino and his two sisters and brother worked together, shining shoes and selling newspapers, doing what they could to get some money. It was hard times, living with no electricity or fresh water.

Palomino's father was a farmer, and he also hauled cotton to put food on the table inside their one room shack they called home. In 1960, they packed up what they had and crossed the border from Tijuana into America.

Carlos went to school and played baseball, with dreams of playing in the major league.

His father loved boxing, and he wanted his sons to box and eventually Palomino would start training and hitting the heavy bag, showing speed and natural athleticism. As time passed, he would spar anyone, including the inmates from the 'Chino' prison in San Bernardino.

Working as a welder, Palomino would then be enlisted into the armed forces where he continued his amateur career, facing future 1972 Olympic gold medallist, Sugar Ray Seales.

Palomino would share and split wins with Seales to then go on and win the All-Army national Championship to become the number one in the United States as a super lightweight, leaving the Military with thirty-five fights and two losses. Palomino turned professional in 1972.

He made his debut in September of that year, winning on points at the Olympic Auditorium in Los Angeles and he was paid one hundred dollars.

Palomino fought his first eight fights, winning on points, and while his style of fighting was aggressive and exciting, he wasn't a devastating puncher in the gym or the ring.

I asked Carlos about his power in his early fights, and he said, "I had fast hands, and I trained very hard, but my punching power took time to develop. I learned to sit down on my punches to generate power. I worked hard in the gym from at first being a boxer, setting a fast pace to win, to then knocking my opponents out".

In 1974, he faced the talented and lightning-fast boxer, Andy 'The Hawk' Price and lost in a close ten round split decision.

Andy Price would fight on, facing Pipino Cuevas, Jose Baquedano, and Sugar Ray Leonard, and also giving everything he had inside, in his fight with Dave Boy Green in London. It was a brilliantly fought battle of sheer will to win from both fighters, but after ten exhausting rounds, Green's hand was raised.

Palomino would fight six times in 1974 and 1975, closing out a hectic schedule with a draw with the veteran, Hedgemon Lewis.

Lewis would challenge the WBC welterweight champion, John H Stracey, in his first defence in 1976 after the fight being postponed due to Stracey being hospitalised and having surgery on his stomach. The fired-up Englishman battered Lewis with spiteful punches across the ring, knocking him out and retaining his title in the tenth round. Lewis never fought again.

In June 1976, Palomino, in his twenty fourth fight, was the number one contender so he crossed over the pond to England to challenge John H Stracey for the title he won in December 1975. Stracey had beaten the legendary Cuban born, Jose Napoles in a bull fighting ring, in his hometown of Mexico City in front of 40,000 hostile fans. Jose Napoles never fought again.

In the fight, Palomino attacked Stracey from the first bell, throwing big right hands to his head, and targeting his body while pushing him back to the ropes. Stracey fought back with heart and courage, landing big right hands of his own, but after being caught with a huge right hand and a sickening body punch in the championship round, he dropped in agony to the canvas. Stracey rose to his feet and Palomino hit him with another body punch that put him down again. The proud and brave champion was hurt badly but he got up, and Palomino opened up with more punches to his head and body that took everything from Stracey. The referee stepped in and stopped the fight in the twelfth round. It was over.

Carlos 'King' Palomino realised his dream of becoming a world champion.

His first defence was against a very tough Armando Muniz.

Known as 'El Hombre', Muniz had challenged Jose Napoles for his world title, twice in 1975, losing the first fight in very controversial circumstances, with Napoles being on the verge of losing and with both eyes swollen and cut, the referee stopped the fight in the twelfth round, saying to the crowd that Napoles won the contest by a technical decision due to the injuries to the champions eyes being caused by Muniz's head butts and not his punches. In the rematch, Napoles beat Muniz.

Palomino could have fought anyone in his first defence, but he took on the tough challenge of Muniz. For 'El Hombre' this was his redemption, his chance to change his family's life and justice for all. In the fight, both Mexican warriors never took a backward step. Muniz knocking Palomino down in the first round. They were like two bulls, locking horns, with neither man willing to concede until the championship rounds, Muniz started to tire, and Palomino opened up with a two-fisted attack on the brave challenger, leaving Muniz to survive while absorbing the onslaught. With just over one minute left in the fifteenth round, Muniz was stopped on his feet.

Palomino returned to London in June 1977 to take on 'The Fenlan Tiger' Dave Boy Green in Wembley. Green was renowned for being in exciting, heart and soul fights. He beat Stracey in the 10th round in March 1977 and he was supremely confident he could beat the champion, Palomino and bring the championship belt back to English soil. Green fought brilliantly, hurting Palomino but he couldn't make a dent in the iron chin of 'The King'.

Palomino started slow, but as the fight went on, he pressured Green with non-stop combinations that took their toll on the face of the Englishman. Palomino battered the eye of Green, and he was finding it hard to see the punches coming and in the tenth round, even though Green buzzed Palomino hard, the writing was on the wall.

Palomino's pressure took everything out of the courageous challenger, knocking him out with a big left hook in the eleventh round. It was a tremendous fight of courage and guts and a memorable win for Palomino.

Dave Boy Green went on to fight Sugar Ray Leonard in 1980, where he was knocked out cold in the fourth round. He retired in 1981.

Palomino defended his title four times to then fight Armando Muniz in an anticipated rematch at the Olympic Auditorium in Los Angeles. Palomino was too strong, aggressive and accurate with his punches. Muniz fought with pride but at the end of the fifteen rounds, Palomino broke his hand but won by a unanimous decision. Armando Muniz retired at the end of 1978, losing to Sugar Ray Leonard in his last fight.

The champion then packed his bags and travelled down to San Juan, Puerto Rico in January 1979, to fight the young, gifted speedster, Wilfred Benitez.

The man known as 'El Radar' had won the WBA junior welterweight world title when he was only seventeen years old, beating the Colombian, Antonio Cervantes in March 1976. Going into his fight with Palomino, Benitez had an unbeaten record of thirty six wins with one draw. He was a special fighter and in the fight, Benitez showed tremendous accuracy, counterpunching, and using his fast hands and quick reflexes, to frustrate the stalking Palomino. The champion came on strong, but Benitez had the fight in the grasp.

After an exciting fight and a brilliant performance from both champions, Benitez won by a split decision. The difference in the fight was the brilliant jab and counter punching by Benitez. Wilfred Benitez fought on until 1990, with a record of 62 fights with 53,wins, 8 losses and 1 draw, fighting legendary fighters in an era of greats.

With little rest, Palomino was back in the gym, and five months later he took on one of the most ferocious lightweights in history, Roberto Duran. The man known as 'Manos De Piedra' had relinquished his undisputed lightweight title to move up to welterweight. Palomino took the fight when many would have said no.

In the fight, Duran was aggressive, and he was out working Palomino on the inside, happy to brawl and prove his strength at the new weight. Duran hit Palomino with a big right hand in the sixth round, knocking him down but he got up quickly to fire back. Palomino was cut to his left ear after taking so many of Duran's right hands.

The champion came back strongly with his own non-stop punching on the inside, but Duran kept coming to win on points at Madison Square Garden.

Carlos Palomino retired immediately after the fight, saying, "I knew it was time. My heart and mind, was not in it anymore."

Palomino left the sport and pursued a career in acting. He also graduated from college with a degree in recreational administration.

In 1996, Palomino made a decision to return to the ring after losing his father to cancer. It was a personal choice made with a heavy heart and as an act of remembrance.

Palomino fought four times in 1997, winning by stoppages.

In 1998, he went looking for a fight with Wilfredo Rivera. The Puerto Rican had shared the ring with Livingstone Bramble, Oscar De La Hoya and Pernell Whitaker on two occasions. Palomino was forty-eight years old. Rivera won the fight on points where it all started, at the Olympic Auditorium in LA.

Carlos Palomino left boxing the way he had come in, as a quiet man with dignity and grace under pressure.

CAREER TOTALS

Palomino retired with a fight record of 31 wins (19 KOs) 4 losses and 3 draws.

CARLOS PALOMINO – A DAY IN THE LIFE

What time did you get up in the morning?

I was up at 5:00 am to run.

How far did you run?

I ran 6 miles every morning at a fast pace. I did 6 miles in 36 minutes.

Did you stretch before you run?

Yes. Full body stretch. I stretched for 20 minutes before and after.

What did you do after your roadwork?

I had breakfast then I had to get to my college classes. I was studying for a degree in recreation park administration when I was boxing.

What time did you go to the gym?

I was at the gym every day at 5:00 pm. I had school and I also had a part time job. I trained for 2 hours, finishing at 7:00 pm. I trained 6 days in the gym.

What did you eat for dinner?

I liked fish or chicken. Vegetables and I liked carrots and Mexican brown beans. I drank Kool-Aid and water.

What did you do for fun?

It was tough. I didn't have much time for anything else. When I won the world title, I quit my job. I had more time with my family and my son. We would go to the park and play baseball and softball.

What job did you do?

I started off, being in the Army. I had a job at a community centre. I would open up the recreation centre for the kids. They would play pool and play football.

What time did you go to bed?

Around 9:00 pm.

NON-SPARRING DAYS

- Warm up / Stretch / Move around. 15 minutes.
- Wrap Hands.
- Shadow Box 4 rounds x 3 minutes with a 1-minute break in between each round.
- Jump Rope 15 minutes non-stop.
- Heavy Bag 4 rounds x 3 minutes with a 1-minute break.
- Double End Bag / Floor to Ceiling Bag 3 rounds x 3 minutes with a 1-minute break between.
- Shadow Box 3 rounds x 3 minutes.

Note: all exercises added up to 18 rounds x 3 minutes.

- Floor exercises.
- Sit ups x 200.
- Push ups x 100.

SPARRING DAYS

- Wrap Hands.
- Warm up / Stretching / Move around 15 minutes.
- Jump Rope 12 minutes.
- Shadow Box 3 rounds x 3 minutes with a 1-minute break in between each round.
- Sparring begins. Always 3 or 4 Sparring Partners waiting.
- 12 rounds x 3 minutes with a 1-minute break in between each round rounds.
- The mindset was, if you could do 12 hard rounds in the gym, you could do 15 rounds in a fight.
- Heavy Bag 3 rounds x 3 minutes with a 1-minute break.
- Speed Bag 3 rounds x 3 minutes with a 1-minute break in between each round.
- Palomino would do 200 rounds of hard Sparring in training for his fights.

To Gary
Best Wishes

STEVE COLLINS

'The Celtic Warrior',
'The Long Hard Road'

BIOGRAPHY

Steve Collins was born in 1964 in Dublin, Ireland. He started boxing as a boy of eight years old, campaigning in an 82 win-8 loss amateur career, winning multiple Irish titles, and representing Ireland many times.

In 1986, Collins was in Yonkers, New York, representing Ireland in an international competition against the USA and he decided then that he wanted to turn professional and with that, while the rest of his amateur team went home, Collins caught the next bus to Boston, Massachusetts to pursue his dream of going to train in Brockton, the 'City of Champions' and the home of heavyweight great, Rocky Marciano, and the current middleweight champion of the world, Marvelous Marvin Hagler.

A stranger in a new land, the twenty-one-year-old boxer was hungry and starving for success and he eventually made his way to Brockton and to the gym of his hero, Marvin Hagler. As he stood at the bottom of the long wooden stairs to the third floor of the Petronelli gym, he knew this was his chance to show what he had, and he knew he would be fighting for his life.

After meeting Pat and Goody Petronelli, it was then decided that Collins would be better suited to fight at middleweight as he was so strong. Collins fought in the amateurs as a light heavyweight.

Collins turned professional in October 1986, fighting and winning in New England on the same undercard as Freddie Roach and Mickey Ward.

Fighting four and five fights a year on the tough undercard circuit of Boston and Philadelphia while still having to pay the bills ultimately meant there was never much time for anything else but training and sleeping. He would run in the morning then go to work as an electrician then as soon as he finished his shift, he would eat then drive the ninety-minute round trip to the gym, train, get home and go to bed. Collins would say, "There was nothing else for me. I was doing this every day, and the training and sparring was brutal. The guys I was fighting were hard men. Every one of them so I had to train harder, and I also wanted to prove I was the man in the gym".

It was Collins mindset, work ethic and discipline that got him through his first sixteen fights, fighting tough desperate and hungry fighters and contenders in Jesse Lanton, Paul McPeek, Kevin Watts, and Tony Thornton.

It was now 1990 and Collins was ranked in the top ten which put him in contention to fight for a world title.

Jamaican body puncher, Mike 'The Body Snatcher' McCallum was the WBA middleweight world champion, and he was looking for a 'keep-'em-busy' fight before he faced the Englishman, Michael Watson and with that, Collins received the news he always knew he would get, and he never hesitated and accepted the challenge with vigour and confidence in his own ability to mix it with the elites at 160 pounds (72.5 kilos).

The fight was held in Boston and the Irish were there in full voice, cheering on their man.

Collins was young and eager to show what he had on the biggest stage, charging McCallum, trying to maul and throw wild combinations on the inside but the experience of McCallum served him well, out boxing the Irishman in the first six rounds.

Collins kept coming and he was relentless, walking through McCallum's counters and body punches, throwing his own right-hand punches that troubled the champion, who in the end decided he had boxed well enough to win the fight, and instead of trading punches with the Irishman, he chose to stick and move until the final bell, winning on points.

Two months later, McCallum would go on to batter Michael Watson in brutal fashion, giving him a long beating to then knock him out in the eleventh round. Watson would fight Chris Eubank the following year, in a fight that ended in tragedy, with Watson collapsing in his corner after a twelfth-round stoppage, after taking unanswered punches from a desperate, behind on points, Eubank.

Watson was in a coma and was left severely disabled with blood clots to his brain.

Collins fought on as he knew his time would come. In 1992, Collins was training back in Ireland, and he was matched to fight the slick and talented southpaw, Reggie Johnson for the vacant WBA middleweight world title. Collins game plan was to pot shot and counter punch the American and bust him up in close quarters. It was a bruising but entertaining and close fight that could have gone either way but in the end, Johnson won by a majority decision.

Six months later, Collins packed his bags and flew to Italy to fight the European champion, and defensive genius and counter puncher, Sumbu Kalambay.

Kalambay was born in the Belgian Congo but moved to Italy as a young boy, and after a great amateur career, he won the European title, out pointing Herol Graham, and then winning the WBA middleweight world title, beating world champion, Iran Barkley, and defending his belt against Mike McCallum, before losing by knockout to Michael Nunn.

For Collins, beating Kalambay, even at this stage of his illustrious career, and winning the European title could get him another chance to fulfil his dream of becoming a world champion so it was worth the trip.

In the fight, there was no doubt why the Italian boxer had the success he had, fighting with superb skill and using every bit of his experience to keep Collins off him. Collins wanted to engage but Kalambay chose the path of least resistance and boxed to a controversial majority decision, leaving the Irishman so near yet so far again.

At that point he could have walked away. Many would have but he continued to fight, to train harder as he had his eyes firmly focused on the UK middleweight scene, as besides the boyhood dream of becoming a world champion, there was also big money fights out there and maybe this time, it was his time.

Collins continued fighting, mostly on Nigel Benn and Chris Eubank undercards, winning by knockout, while waiting for his moment in time, and in 1994, Collins challenged the English boxer, Chris Pyatt for the WBO middleweight championship of the world and this time, he made no mistake of leaving it to the judges, knocking out Pyatt in the fifth round to become champion of the world.

All the sacrifices, leaving his home and family in Ireland, the hard years in Boston, the disappointment of losing in close fights were things that couldn't be forgotten and now as a champion, he would need to embrace those bitter memories in time and use it to fuel the fire as now, everyone wanted what he had. Collins was now thirty-one years old and after having three fights fall apart, he made the move to jump up in weight to super middleweight and challenge the WBO champion, Chris Eubank. Collins said, "I was really struggling to make 160 and I just couldn't get big money fights and Eubank was the biggest star in the UK and he was a 43 fight, unbeaten world champion and I knew I could beat him. It was an easy move".

The fight with Eubank was staged on St Patrick Day weekend at the Green Glens Arena, Millstreet, County Cork, Ireland and as Eubank was getting caught up in a busy schedule of media and TV, Collins isolated himself in his Las Vegas training camp. The build up to the fight was unbelievable, with Collins arriving to the press conference dressed as an Irish laird, accompanied by an Irish wolfhound. He made the champion wait for forty-five minutes on him and he would only speak in his Irish Gaelic tongue, and he purposely acted strange, staring out Eubank. There was talk of Collins being hypnotised so he wouldn't feel any pain, and that he would keep punching without getting tired. This visibly unsettled Eubank and Collins gave the master of mind games something to think about.

Come fight night, Collins was so fired up to be the first man to beat the brilliant and brash Eubank. The bell rang and it was on. Collins told me, "All that talk of being hypnotised and not feeling pain...every punch he threw hurt me. His body shots hurt. His punches to my head hurt. He was so tough that I knew it was going to be my toughest fight yet, but I couldn't let him see I was hurt or tired and I kept the pressure on, taking one from him and timing him so I could land two and I had to fight the same way in round one all the way till the end. I knocked him down in the eighth round and he got me in the tenth and we traded punches until the final bell. It was hell but I knew I had won."

Collins beat Eubank by a unanimous decision to become the new WBO super middleweight champion of the world and a two-weight champion.

In the dressing room after the fight, Collins temperature rose dangerously high, and paramedics were called in and they covered his body in ice, and he was put on oxygen for extreme exhaustion.

After all the years in boxing, the politics, the setbacks, Collins was on top of the world and big money fights were on the horizon. Eubank struggled with defeat, and it was seen by many that Eubank had a bad night, and it was a huge upset, and all the talk was for a rematch.

Eubank v Collins 2 was a fight that had to happen. Eubank had had his ego dented, and his pride rattled, and he wanted revenge. For Collins, the fight would make him financially secure, and he gave Eubank the same opportunity that he gave him.

Collins trained hard with his old friend, Freddie Roach as his trainer and in the rematch, Collins fought like a man possessed, a lunatic, running out the corner, throwing wild shots at Eubank, not letting him breathe as he buried his head on the former champions chest and banged away with no regard or respect for Eubank's ability or his power.

Eubank couldn't settle and Collins wouldn't give him the time or space to fight his fight. With blood pouring down his face, Collins finished strongly and retained his title by a surprising split decision. Eubank fought on, but really, he was never the same, losing to Joe Calzaghe and Carl Thompson, finally hanging up the gloves in July 1998.

After a short break, Collins was back in training to fight the talented Cornelius Carr.

Carr had been one of Roy Jones main sparring partners prior to the fight and he took the fight at short notice but lost on points in Dublin. Carr would then go on to win the WBF title, beating Steve Foster and former world champion, 'The Rose of Soweto',

Dingaan Thobela.

Collins was defending his title, and he was making good money but all he wanted now was the fight that was talked about for years. Nigel Benn.

Benn was a fearsome force in the middleweight division and every time he fought, he was so unpredictable that you just never knew what you would get. He was most dangerous when he was hurt, and he would be wobbled or down to then get up to stop his opponents in exciting fashion. He was a tough no nonsense man who trusted no one. He was aptly named 'The Dark Destroyer'.

In February 1995, Benn took on the challenge of the American puncher, Gerald McClellan and he would be fighting as a betting underdog, with no one giving him a chance of winning.

Mc Clellan was a power punching force and had been since beating and taking John 'The Beast' Mugabi's WBO middleweight title in 1991, to then go on and knock out one of the biggest punchers in the division, Julian Jackson, and take his WBC middleweight title in 1993. He was a mean street-kid from the hood who had been sparring in wars at the Kronk gym for years. In the walk out, billed as 'Sudden Impact', McClellan walked to the ring with a calm arrogance and a menacing demeanour while Benn was ranting and roaring while bouncing and shadow boxing, raring to go.

In the fight, McClellan wasted no time battering Benn to the ropes in the first round, and after a flurry of punches, he knocked Benn through the ropes. Benn came back and somehow held on. In round two, Benn was ducking low, very low and he managed to get his legs moving, and back into the fight. It was shear heart and the will to not just survive, but to win. In the eighth round, Benn was caught again with a big right hand and his legs dipped and it seemed this was the end, but Benn came back again like a wounded lion throwing lunging punches that troubled the American. It was an unbelievable display of heart and courage. From there on, McClellan started showing signs that something was wrong. He was pushing his gum Shield out and was noticeably blinking while throwing punches. He was winning the fight but in the tenth round, after being hit in the back of the head, he took a knee twice then staring down at the canvas, he was blinking repeatedly and made no attempt to rise, and the referee counted him out. McClellan immediately rose to his feet and walked to his corner and sat down on the ring apron.

McClellan was taken to the hospital where he fell into a coma and had to be operated on to remove blood clots from his brain.

McClellan sustained serious brain damage. He has lost his sight, is partially deaf, and has also lost the ability to walk unaided.

Benn fought on and defended his title twice but was beaten in 1996 on a close split decision by the South African, Thulani 'Sugar Boy' Malinga.

After all the talk, the Benn fight was signed for the 6th of July 1996, and Steve Collins prepared and trained hard in Jersey while Nigel Benn got himself ready for war in Tenerife and both men left no stone unturned in training.

The fight was fought at the Nynex Arena in Manchester and the atmosphere was electric and expectations were high from the sold-out crowd.

Collins countered Benn all night and was just too strong pushing him back to the ropes and throwing wide looping punches and uppercuts with his right hand finding a home every time he threw it, forcing the faded 'Destroyer' to throw lunging, wild punches, that missed, leaving Benn on the canvas with a twisted ankle and a forced retirement in the centre of the ring.

Benn had always fought courageously, and no one could question his huge heart. In the end, the granite-chinned Collins style negated Benn's.

It was a disappointing way for the fight to finish with many fight fans left feeling cheated so although unnecessary, it was announced that there would be a rematch. Four months later, 'Judgement Day' was on.

Collins handed Benn a one-sided beating in Manchester, with Benn's corner stopping their fighter from taking anymore punishment at the end of the sixth round. Nigel Benn never fought again.

There was talk of Collins fighting Roy Jones Jnr., and the timing was right, but in the end, it was just talk. Collins fought twice in 1997, winning by stoppage, but he was struggling to find meaningful opponents to fight him, to challenge him, to scare him and motivate him to train hard in camp. He had been on a long hard road for many years and now it was time.

CAREER TOTALS

After achieving so much in his life in boxing, The Celtic Warrior walked away with a hit record of 36 wins (21 KOs), 3 losses and no draws.

What time did you get up in the morning?

7:00 am to run. If I was in Los Angeles or Las Vegas, I would get up at 6:00 am to run. In the years I was training in Boston, I would run earlier as I had to go to work. I did my roadwork then I went to work.

How far did you run?

I did different runs to break it up. I would run 5 miles during the week and at the weekends, I would run 6 mile runs.

Did you stretch?

Never ever.

What did you do after your run?

I would eat. Rest a bit. Make a few phone calls. I would sort out my gym gear and I always had to sort out my food.

What did you eat for breakfast?

I would have oatmeal, yogurt, cup of tea and water.

What did you do after breakfast?

I would drive to work. It was hard going but there was no choice.

How many days did you train in the gym?

6 days with Sunday off. I would run in the morning. Work all day as a qualified city and guilds electrician. I worked in the Local 103 union in Boston. I finished work and I would drive to Brockton to train or spar. You never knew if you were sparring until you got there.

What was your favourite exercise in the gym?

Sparring.

What time did you go to the gym?

7:00 pm until 9:00 pm. I would then drive home from Brockton.

What did you eat for dinner?

I prepared my food in the morning, and I ate at 4:30 pm at work. I had basic meat, potatoes and make a sandwich, and I would drink a gallon of water every day.

What did you do for fun?

Those days in Massachusetts, there wasn't much time for anything. I was on a mission to be a champion of the world and that's all I had in my mind. On Sundays, I took my daughter to Castle Island in Boston, and we would have a good time. We would eat dessert, and I would have a beer. It was good for the brain.

What jobs did you do?

I worked in the Guinness brewery factory in Dublin. I worked as a labourer in Boston. I also worked in a bar, pulling pints.

What time did you go to bed?

10:30 pm.

NON-SPARRING DAYS

Monday, Wednesday and Friday

- 7:00 pm – 9:00 pm.
- Wrap Hands.
- Loosen up / Warm up / Move around. 15 minutes.
- Shadow Box 3 rounds x 3 minutes with a 1-minute break in between each round.
- Focus Mitts 4 rounds x 3 minutes with a 1-minute rest between each round.
- Heavy Bag 4 rounds x 3 minutes with a 1-minute break between each round.
- Floor exercises – core work.
- Sit ups x 300 always 300.
- Press ups / push ups x 100.
- Leg raises x 100.
- Skipping 15 minutes non-stop.
- 4:30 pm.

Twice a week, Collins would do a session of Heavy weight training before going to the boxing gym at 7:00 pm. He included this to add power to his arsenal.

SPARRING DAYS

- 7:00 pm – 9:00 pm.
- Wrap Hands.
- Loosen up / Warm up / Moving around. 15 minutes.
- Shadow Box 3 rounds x 3 minutes with a 1-minute break in between each round.
- Sparring begins : Collins would say, "There were always hard hungry fighters there to spar. Robbie Sims was always there. There was boxers in training for a fight or the Olympic trials. As soon as you got in there, you had to be ready for a war. It was tough. You never knew who you would be sparring and if you would be sparring until you climbed up those long wooden stairs to the gym".
- Sparring 6 x rounds x 3-minute rounds with a 1-minute break between each round. As the fight got closer, the rounds increased to 8 rounds then 10 rounds. The mindset was, if you could do 10 hard rounds in the gym, you could do 12 rounds in the fight.

FLOOR WORK

- Sit ups x 300.
- Press ups / push ups x 100.
- Leg raises x 100.
- Skipping 15 minutes non-stop.

MIKE WEAVER

'Baptism of Fire'

BIOGRAPHY

Mike Weaver was born in 1951 in the small town of Gatesville, Texas.

He was a talented, athletic, seventeen-year-old when he enlisted into the Marine corps in 1968 in the final years of the war in Vietnam.

Weaver began boxing in the amateurs while serving in the armed forces, competing in twenty-six contests with three losses. Weaver wasn't at all interested in boxing but after knocking out a Marine heavyweight champion with one punch in a bar room altercation, he was encouraged to compete as a fighting Marine. Weaver won the All-Marine title, and the All-Services title, to then fight in the Golden Gloves tournaments.

After his time in the Marines ended, Weaver turned professional in 1972, fighting across California, San Diego, Reno, Los Angeles, and San Francisco. He would fight anyone, anytime, and winning and losing was just part of the fight game. In 1974, after training and sparring with Ken Norton, the two boxers had a special bond, as Marine Corp champions, Norton encouraged Weaver to train hard and work hard as he saw something special in him. Norton called him 'Hercules' and he would take this into the ring with him every time he fought.

This was the turning point for Weaver.

He trained with conviction, and he listened to Norton as he respected him as a friend and for his courage in the ring.

Norton had fought Muhammad Ali in 1973, wearing 10-oz gloves, breaking Ali's jaw to win a close split decision in San Diego, to then face him in a rematch in the same year, losing in another close split decision.

Norton then challenged the powerful puncher, George Foreman (39 wins, 0 losses) in early 1974, for his WBC and WBA Heavyweight Championship of the world, where he was knocked down three times by hard brutal punches, knocking Norton out in the second round in Venezuela.

Weaver fought the experienced and dangerous Rodney Bobick, losing on points, to then face his undefeated hard punching brother, (23 wins, 0 losses) Duane Bobick in San Diego, losing by knockout in the seventh round.

Despite losing, Weaver continued to train hard, sparring anyone he could including George Foreman, Ron Lyle and Muhammad Ali.

Weaver fought another eleven fights, losing two to then face the hard punching

Colombian, Bernardo Mercado (20 wins, 1 loss) in 1978, fighting fire with fire, knocking him out in the fifth round.

Weaver then went on a knockout winning streak, which earned him a shot at the undefeated (30 wins, 0 losses) WBC champion, Larry Holmes.

The fight was held in New York and with only three weeks to get ready, no one gave Weaver a chance.

In the fight, the twenty-nine-year-old Holmes used his fast hard jab and thudding clubbing punches, but Weaver kept coming forward, forcing the champion back and landing some big punches on the champions chin and body. Holmes was exhausted and hurt, but he found a way back, and with Weaver showing fatigue, the champion decked him with a perfect right uppercut in the eleventh round. With ten seconds to go in the round, Weaver rose and walked back to his corner on unsteady legs. He had given everything, and he fought his heart out. In the twelfth round, Holmes jumped from his stool and unleashed his jab and right hand and uppercuts, until the referee stepped in to end the fight. It was a tremendously gruelling heavyweight fight for the ages.

Larry Holmes would continue on to a forty-eight fight, unbeaten run until 1985, where he was beaten on points by Michael Spinks. 'The Easton Assassin' fought them all, retiring in 2002.

Hercules came back with two good wins. That earned him a shot at the former Olympian, and WBA champion, John Tate in his hometown of Knoxville, Tennessee.

Going into the fight, Tate was unbeaten, and he had knocked out Bernardo Mercado and Duane Bobick, to then go to South Africa to beat the (23 wins, 0 losses) champion, Gerrie Coetzee on points to become the heavyweight champion of the world. Weaver was knocking his sparring partners out in the gym, but he was once again the underdog.

In the fight, the champion and challenger slugged it out, round after round, with the 6'4 Tate firing hard combinations to Weaver's head and body. Weaver never stopped coming forward, taking Tate's best punches, and fighting back off the ropes. Weaver gritted his teeth and fought with a brave heart, taking huge punches from the champion until, the fifteenth round, and needing a knockout to win, he mauled Tate inside, and threw a thunderbolt short left hook that sent the champion, face first to the canvas where he lay with his eyes closed and unable to move. Mike Weaver was the WBA heavyweight champion of the world. Nothing ever came easy, but he defied the odds through an unwavering self-belief and also his faith in God.

"At the end of the fourteenth round, I knew I only had three minutes to knock this guy out. I sat there and I asked the lord to give me the strength to knock him out. I recited the twenty third Psalm in my head, and I got off my stool and knocked him out. The Lord answered my prayer."

Tate fought on and he was knocked out a few months later in the ninth round by Trevor Berbick, to then go on a long unbeaten run, retiring after being beaten in his last fight in 1988.

Weaver travelled to South Africa to fight the hard punching Gerrie Coetzee (23 wins, 1 loss) in his first defence in 1980 and to many, it was an unpopular choice to go and fight there as there was tension and unrest with apartheid and there was violence in the shanty towns and the streets.

Weaver was confident he could beat 'The Boksburg Bomber' in his own backyard. The South African had knocked out Leon Spinks but was beaten by Tate on points. Weaver trained hard, busting up his sparring partners and going into the fight in peak condition.

The fight was another tough fight. Coetzee was a proud, stubborn fighter who had never been down, and he could relieve any one of his opponents' senses in any round. Weaver pressured and pushed while trying to find the knockout, but in the eighth round, the South African caught him with a right hand that hurt Weaver, shaking him to his boots, hitting him so hard that he saw three of Coetzee in the ring, but he took his best punch to come back and knock out Coetzee in the thirteenth round to retain his title in a tremendous hard fought victory in Sun City.

Coetzee fought on, facing Michael Dokes, Pinklon Thomas, Greg Page, James Tillis, Frank Bruno, and Iran Barkley in his last fight in 1997.

After beating the undefeated (20 wins, 0 losses) James 'Quick' Tillis over fifteen rounds on points, Weaver went to Las Vegas to fight another undefeated fighter, Michael 'Dynamite' Dokes in December 1982.

In the lead up to the fight, the sport of boxing was in a state of shock and sadness as the South Korean lightweight contender, Duk Koo Kim died after being stopped in the fourteenth round by the WBA world champion, Ray Mancini in Las Vegas in the November. He was twenty-seven years old.

It was a tragedy, and it was so raw and real that it highlighted how dangerous boxing could be as a sport.

The TV networks and the promoters were nervous, and they were scrambling to find a way to protect their investments. The WBC made a statement that they would introduce a maximum of twelve rounds for their world title fights, moving forward and they urged the other sanctioning bodies to follow their lead. The Weaver v Dokes WBA world title fight was scheduled for fifteen rounds.

In the fight, the two fighters met in the centre of the ring, and they exchanged punches with bad intentions. It was fast and furious with the champion being caught, going down early from a left hook. Weaver got up quickly and wasn't hurt. He was historically known as a slow starter. The champion was pushed back to the ropes where Dokes opened up with an onslaught of head and body punches that had the champion bringing his arms up, protecting himself and waiting for the chance to punch his way off the ropes. That chance never came for him as the referee stepped in at 1:57 seconds of the first round and stopped the fight and raised Dokes hand in victory. It was a controversial fight.

The rematch was signed for May 1983 in the heat of the Las Vegas sun.

In the fight, Weaver was more aggressive, going to the body and using his jab, while stalking Dokes, and with the champion content on doubling up with the jab and coasting through the rounds and looking exhausted from the ninth round on, it seemed Weaver would box his way to victory and regain his title.

After fifteen rounds, the judges scored the fight 145–141, 144–144, and 143–143 – a majority draw.

Dokes fought on, losing his WBA title later that year, being knocked out by Gerrie Coetzee. He retired in 1997 after a long hard career, fighting Randall Cobb, Evander Holyfield, Razor Ruddock, and Riddick Bowe.

In 1985, Weaver challenged the 25 wins, 0 losses, 1 draw, Pinklon Thomas for the WBC belt but was knocked out in the eighth round in Las Vegas. He came back with a knockout win over the talented (17 wins, 1 loss) Carl Williams to then be beaten by James 'Bonecrusher' Smith and Donovan Ruddock.

After a fifteen-year career, he travelled back to South Africa to face the hard-as-nails brawler, (17 wins, 0 losses) Johnny Du Plooy, winning the fight due to the South African injuring his wrist.

The two met five months later in Sun City, with Du Plooy knocking Weaver out with a huge right hand in the second round in 1988.

Weaver fought on, facing 'Bonecrusher' Smith, Lennox Lewis, Bert Cooper, and at forty-nine years old, he ended his 28-year career, fighting Larry Holmes in 2000, losing by a six-round stoppage in Biloxi, Mississippi.

Mike Hercules Weaver travelled to Canada, China, South Africa, Alaska, and he fought anyone who would fight him all across America. He had his faith and his family and he drew strength from them to be the best he could be to become the heavyweight champion of the world.

CAREER TOTALS

Mike Hercules Weaver retired with 41 wins (28 KOs), 18 losses (12 KOs) and 1 draw.

MIKE WEAVER

MIKE WEAVER – A DAY IN THE LIFE

What time did you get up?

6:00 am every morning.

Did you do your roadwork in the morning?

Yes. I ran 4 miles every day.

Did you stretch out before you run?

Yes. I did a lot of stretching. I also did push ups, leg squats.

What did you do after running?

I showered then I ate.

What did you eat for breakfast?

Eggs, bacon, corn bread, oatmeal, fruits, juices.

What did you do after breakfast?

I rested my body, and I watched TV for 2 hours.

What time did you go to the gym?

4:00 pm. I finished up at 6:00 pm every day.

What was your favourite exercise in the gym?

I liked punching the heavy bag and I liked hitting the speed bag. I wouldn't say I enjoyed this, but I would do 500 sit ups, 3 times a day, every day.

How many days in the gym?

I trained 6 days, with Sunday off.

What did you eat for dinner?

I liked steak, chicken, fish and potatoes, vegetables. I liked salads and I would drink fruit juices and water.

What did you do for fun or a hobby?

I liked to play the slot machines in the casinos. I liked watching the TV. I really enjoy playing the piano.

What job did you do?

I worked as a maintenance man at a school. I worked in a post office, and I worked in a store.

What time did you go to sleep?

I would go to bed around 10:00 pm.

NON-SPARRING DAYS

- Jump Rope 30 minutes non-stop.
- Body Stretching exercises 10 minutes.
- Hit the Heavy Bag 6–8 rounds x 3 minutes with a 1-minute break after each round.
- Speed Bag 4 rounds x 3 minutes with a 1-minute rest between rounds.
- Jump rope (again) 15 minutes non-stop.
- Push ups 3 x 50.
- Sit ups x 500.
- Sauna and Steam after workout. Casual swimming to relax and loosen up.

SPARRING DAYS

- Wrap hands.
- Jump Rope 20 minutes.
- Body stretching/ warming up 10 minutes.
- Shadow Box 3 rounds x 3 minutes with a 1-minute break between rounds.
- (Sparring begins – there is always 3 or 4 sparring partners waiting to spar.)
- 10 rounds of hard sparring 10 x 3-minute rounds with a 1-minute break between rounds.
- Hit the Heavy Bag 3 rounds x 3 minutes with a 1-minute break between rounds.
- Speed Bag 2 rounds x 3 minutes.
- Jump Rope (again) 15 minutes non-stop.
- Floor exercises Sit ups x 500 to finish workout.
- Mike would do 3 sets x 500 sit ups, spread across the day – morning, afternoon and night.

CLETO
REYES

ANGEL

BIOGRAPHY

Angel Manfredy was born in October 1974. A son to Puerto Rican parents, and born and bred in the tough, industrial 'Steel City' of Gary, Indiana.

Manfredy started boxing when he was nine years old and competed in fifty-six contests as an amateur. He turned professional in 1993 at the age of eighteen.

It was clear that Manfredy had ability and a talent for boxing. He moved well, and he had great balance, and his jab was sharp, and fast, and he carried power in both hands.

With his professional career in its infancy, Manfredy was involved in a serious car crash, driving head on into a telegraph pole that left him with 265 stitches in his forehead. Manfredy had been partying with his friends, and he had been drinking heavily and using cocaine. The inebriated Angel was euphoric and with his brain speeding up inside, and the rain pouring down outside, and a cocktail glass in his hand, he put the foot down and drove straight into blind oblivion, crashing to a violent end at the side of the road.

Unbelievably, Manfredy was back fighting six months later, winning and living life the only way he knew, which was on the edge.

Manfredy was training, and boxing and he was enjoying a twenty-three-fight unbeaten run, and, in between his fights, he was living life in the fast lane, like he had some kind of a death wish, which was fuelled by cocaine, alcohol and his self-ego and reputation as a hell raiser.

Manfredy feared no one, winning the WBU super featherweight championship in 1995 against the experienced and tough Calvin Grove, stopping him in the seventh round.

Going into the fight, Grove had beaten John 'The Eastern Beast' Brown and he had shared the ring with greats, Azumah Nelson, Lester Ellis, Jorge Paez, and Jeff Fenech.

Manfredy then travelled to South Africa to fight the southpaw, Mthobeli Mhlophe, knocking him out in the fifth round, to then return to Atlantic City to face the stiff challenge of Wilson Rodriguez of the Dominican Republic. Rodriguez was a tough, durable fighter who had travelled the world, fighting anyone to make a living. He had fast hands with a long reach, and he could fight.

He lost to Arturo Gatti in the six round of their fight in 1996, but he took Gatti's best punches, and he gave him hell, knocking him down in the second round, and taking the Canadian brawler into deep water to then succumb to a sharp left hook to the body and a barrage of punches to end proceedings.

In the fight, Manfredy fought brilliantly, outboxing Rodriguez, winning the rounds and taking his heart to beat him by a unanimous decision.

Six months later, Manfredy knocked out the hard-as-nails showman, Jorge 'El Maromero' Paez in seven rounds which catapulted him into a huge fight with Arturo Gatti in Atlantic City.

Going into the fight, Gatti was 29–1, and he had relinquished his IBF super featherweight world title due to him struggling to boil down to make the weight. He decided to move up to 135lbs, with many believing he would be too much and too strong for Manfredy at the new weight. Manfredy trained harder than ever and going into the fight as a big underdog, he knew everything was stacked against him, but he was strong at the weight.

When they met, Manfredy whispered into Gatti's ear, "I'm going to knock you down, I'm going to cut you and I'm going to beat you. You're not going the distance".

In the fight, Manfredy fought the fight of his life, boxing brilliantly, using his jab with laser-like accuracy, opening a bad cut to the tough Canadian's left eye, in the first round.

Gatti, jabbing and pushing forward as the aggressor, in round two, with Manfredy waiting and watching for the opening.

In the third round, Manfredy was sharp shooting Gatti with accurate punches then, Bang! Gatti went down from a perfect left hook. Gatti was hurt but he got up quickly and fought back well. Gatti pressed forward in the fifth round, but he was being outboxed by Manfredy, despite 'El Diablo', breaking his right hand on Gatti's head.

Manfredy hit Gatti with a big right hand that hurt him to his damaged eye in the seventh round.

In the eighth, Manfredy was boxing, watching and waiting while moving and was connecting with hard punches that Gatti didn't see coming and the referee paused the fight to have a look at his ripped eye. Gatti's corner stepped in and stopped the fight, near the end of the round. Gatti received thirteen stitches on the outside and seven on the inside. Manfredy took Gatti's thunder, but he couldn't take his heart. After his early years, thinking he wasn't good enough, believing he was dumb, growing up with little self-esteem, Manfredy proved, that when focused, on any given night, he was good enough to mix it with the best in the world.

Arturo Gatti fought on in more blood and guts, career defining fights against Ivan Robinson, and his three unforgettable fights with Micky Ward which will go down in the history books as one of the greatest trilogies ever. Arturo Thunder Gatti retired in 2007.

He died in 2009 at the age of thirty-seven.

It was now 1998, and Manfredy was in line to fight in big money fights and at twenty-three years old, he was one of the most entertaining, memorable and exciting boxers in the world.

He had beaten 'The Eastern Beast' John Brown in impressive fashion by a unanimous decision which set up a huge money fight with the undefeated,18-win-fighter from Grand rapids, Michigan, Pretty Boy Floyd Mayweather. Going in, Manfredy had to starve himself and boil himself down in camp to make the weight.

In the fight, Manfredy pressed hard, trying to out-muscle Mayweather, but the footwork and speed was evident, and his single punches were setting the pace of the fight. Every time Manfredy tried to land his combinations, Mayweather countered and slipped out of harm's way. In the second round, Mayweather was going to the body and throwing the one two range finder then he hit Manfredy with a big right hand that hurt him in the centre of the ring. Mayweather attacked, forcing Manfredy to retreat to the corner to then throw twenty-nine unanswered punches to the head of 'El Diablo' with the referee stepping in to end the fight.

Mayweather moved on and became one of the greatest fighters in the history of the sport.

Manfredy fought on and was back in the gym getting ready to fight the 'Mighty' Ivan Robinson at lightweight. He did his roadwork, and he trained and sparred hard as he knew that Robinson always come to fight. Going into the fight, Robinson had beaten Arturo Gatti twice on points, in 1998. The Philadelphia fighter was a tough and skilled boxer, and he had shown courage and the will to win in his twenty-nine-fight career.

I met Manfredy while he was training for Ivan Robinson in 1999, and as I watched him workout, I remember thinking how crazed and focused he looked in the gym. He was peaking as a fighter.

In the fight, Manfredy boxed superbly behind the jab, going to the body of the bigger Robinson with three punch combinations. Robinson came back and never stopped coming forward, making it a war inside in the fast-paced fight. In the end, Manfredy was more accurate, and he put on a superb display of boxing, going to the body and the head of Robinson to win by a unanimous decision.

Manfredy would then fight the talented lightweight, Stevie Johnston, losing on points. Manfredy fought well in a brilliant hard-fought-for fight, but Johnston was just that bit better. The quicker boxer used angles and movement, counterpunching Manfredy from his southpaw stance, landing more accurate punches to win by a unanimous decision.

After the fight, Manfredy partied like it was 1999, going on a crazy train to nowhere on a diet of cocaine and alcohol that almost killed him. Manfredy was on his knees, out of his mind in a darkened room when he heard a voice inside, saying to him, "Are you going to give your life to me, or are you going to take your own?"

Manfredy believes this was a message of love from the lord and it was so profound and hard hitting to him, sending him on a journey of being reborn in a new world and a better life.

El Diablo was gone.

Manfredy had always trained harder than anyone. He was now rejuvenated, and he was happy inside. Manfredy fought seven times in 2000, winning six.

He fought the 32 win, 0 losses Diego 'Chico' Corrales and was beaten by the IBF champion at 130lbs.

Manfredy had to boil and kill himself to make the weight. Corrales was huge at the weight, and he was a big puncher with a huge heart.

In the fight, Manfredy had to get inside and bang to Corrales thin body. Manfredy had great success, thumping big hooks into the liver of Corrales. Corrales stalked and waited for the opportunity to counter, and he landed a short powerful left hook that sent Manfredy down. Manfredy took a big shot but rose to his feet quickly. Corrales opened up on Manfredy with hooks, overhand rights, uppercuts, and body punches, ending the round with a straight right hand.

Manfredy rallied hard and fought bravely, showing a granite chin, taking hard punches from Corrales, while trying to get past his strong jab.

In the third round, the courageous Manfredy charged at Corrales and landed a burst of spectacular punches that Corrales acknowledged by smiling at the smaller man. Corrales then hit Manfredy with a left hook that slammed into the side of his head, making his legs dip and wobble and his body stumbling, with his glove touching the canvas, scoring another knockdown. Corrales was relentless in attack, connecting with twenty-five unanswered punches to end the fight.

Manfredy had taken a beating.

He came back again, winning six in a row, beating the unbeaten Julio Diaz to then challenge 'The Pittsburgh Kid', Paul Spadafora in 2002

Spadafora was the unbeaten 34–0, IBF lightweight champion of the world, and once again Manfredy would go into his opponent's back yard to fight. In the fight, the champion boxed his way to win by a unanimous decision. Spadafora fought on until 2014.

Manfredy fought on but the devil inside had left him.

He left boxing in 2004 after fighting a combined twenty-year amateur and professional career.

He lives happily as 'The Lord's Foot Soldier'.

CAREER TOTALS

Angel Manfredy had a record of 52 fights,
with 43 wins (32 KOs), 8 losses (4 KOs) and 1 draw.

"I WAS BORN TO FIGHT. I FOUND BOXING AND I NEVER LIKED TO LOSE. I WANTED TO PROVE TO MY FAMILY AND EVERYONE THAT I COULD BECOME THE CHAMPION OF THE WORLD."

ANGEL MANFREDY

What time did you get up in the morning?

8:00 am every morning.

Did you do your roadwork in the morning?

No. I ran at 7:00 pm. I ran 3 miles.

Did you stretch out before you ran?

Yes. Full body stretch.

What did you eat for breakfast?

Eggs, bacon, some toast and juice and water.

What did you do after breakfast?

I would relax and get ready and prepared to go to the gym.

What time did you go to the gym?

I would get to the gym at midday and train hard until 2:00 pm.

How many days did you train?

6 days. Sunday off.

What was your favourite exercise in the gym?

I liked to hit the mitts, and I loved sparring.

What did you eat for dinner?

I liked eating pasta. Steak. High-protein food. I drank water.

What did you do for fun when you were in training camp?

Boxing was my hobby. In camp, all you thought about was your training and the fight.

Did you ever have a job?

No. I was boxing since I was nine years old and just kept going. I turned pro at eighteen and I started making some money, so I didn't need a job.

What time did you go to bed?

Around 9:30 pm. Never any later than 10:00 pm.

NON-SPARRING DAYS

- Warm up / Stretching / Moving. 20 minutes total.
- Side to sides.
- Torso twists.
- Touch toes / stretch back and neck.
- Shadow Box 10 rounds x 3 minutes with a 1-minute rest between each round.
- Hit the focus mitts 5 rounds x 3 Minutes with a 1-minute rest between rounds.
- Hit the Heavy Bag 4 rounds x 3 minutes with a 1-minute rest between rounds.
- Jab Bag (Double end bag) 4 rounds x 3-minute rounds with a 1-minute rest between rounds.
- Speed Bag 3 rounds x 3 minutes.
- Jump Rope 30 minutes non-stop.
- Sit ups x 200.
- Push ups x 100.

SPARRING DAYS

4 days a week

- Warm up / light stretching / moving and wrapping hands. 20 minutes total.
- Shadow Box 5 rounds x 3 minutes with a 1-minute rest between rounds.
- Sparring begins. 3 Sparring partners. Manfredy would wear a lot of sparring partners out in training camp as he was ferocious and relentless.
- Sparring 10 rounds x 3 minutes with 1-minute breaks between each round.
- Jab Bag Hit the bag for 4 rounds with a 1-minute rest between each round.
- Speed Bag 4 rounds x 3 minutes with a 1-minute rest between each round.
- Jump Rope 30 minutes non-stop.
- Sit ups x 200.
- Push ups x 100.

Manfredy would swim and shadow box in the pool.

No sauna or massage.

DEONTAY WILDER

'Tuscaloosa's son'

BIOGRAPHY

Deontay Wilder was born in 1985 in the rough and ragged west end of Tuscaloosa, Alabama. Wilder's mother took off when he was nine years old, leaving his father to care for their splintered family.

Wilder went to school, and he excelled in all sports. He loved football, basketball, and running and he dreamed of the day when he could make it big and move his family away from the run-down part of town, and a better life.

Working in IHOP serving pancakes was a means to an end and for Wilder, there was no choice. Wilder was never going to get a college degree or scholarship but what he did have was his own PHD: (He was Poor, Hungry and Driven).

Wilder walked under the steel roller door of the Skyy boxing gym where he introduced himself to Jay Deas, telling him he wanted to box. After a few months of watching the 6'7 Wilder in the gym, Deas saw something in him. He saw a nineteen-year-old boy turn into a man. He was driven and hungry to learn and he wanted to win.

After training hard every day, being the first in the gym and the last one to leave, Wilder fought in forty-three amateur fights, losing five contests, and winning the bronze medal in the 2008 Beijing Olympic Games.

Wilder decided to turn professional immediately after the games, as he was desperate to earn some money. For Wilder it was much more than that. He had to get money quickly to pay for expensive medical bills for his daughter who had been diagnosed with Spina Bifida. Wilder told Deas to get him five-hundred-dollar fights and four-hundred-dollar-fights, telling him he would fight every day to get the money.

As a family man myself, Deontay Wilder's struggle touched me as being such an inspirational story.

I wanted to meet the man behind the story.

It was a story of hope, of perseverance, determination and a love for his family.

I packed my bag, and I headed off on a quest to track down Wilder in his gym in Tuscaloosa. My goal was to go and meet and train and spend as much time as possible with him.

When I boarded the plane in Sydney, Australia, I was filled with mixed emotions of nerves and excitement and as I looked out the window, I thought to myself – *What the hell am I doing?*.

I had done this before, but this time was different. I was going in blind and half-cooked, with absolutely no idea where I was going and no one to contact when I got there. I was on my own on a journey into the unknown.

After thirty-two hours, on three planes, and a ninety-minute taxi ride, I arrived at my hotel in Tuscaloosa. I checked in to my digs but can't remember doing so.

The next morning, I was up and out, armed with a plan to track down Wilder. I had a sketch of where Wilder's gym was in an area called Northport and I started walking. Funny thing about Tuscaloosa is that taxis are non-existent, and the streets are deserted. I asked the locals for directions and as I walked over a road bridge, I took a left and walked under an old railway bridge that looked like something out of a Huckleberry Finn film.

As I walked, I tried to imagine what this area would have looked like, hundreds of years ago. Choctaw Indians running around, hunting and fishing and living off the land, and later, African Americans working in the fields, picking cotton as the sun beat down on them.

I took another left up a long dirt track which had a sign saying '30th Avenue' and I kept walking until I saw a young boy on his bike, and I asked him if he knew where Wilder's gym was. He looked at me and said nothing but pointed. I kept going and turned down towards a huge industrial tin shed. The shed had numbers on each door, and I was looking for the number nine. I walked to the end of the dirt track, and I saw a sign above a roller door saying 'Parking reserved for Mr Wilder. Do not park here.'

I had made it, but the only problem was other than a few wild cats wandering around, there was no one there. It was getting cold, and the sun was going down, so I decided to walk back quick smart.

The next morning I walked back and forth to the gym four times but again, there was no sign of life. I got back to my hotel, and I spoke to the lady on the front desk about getting a taxi. I explained why I had come to Tuscaloosa. She told me that it wasn't a good idea to be walking in that area as it was close to the projects on the other side, and it could be a dangerous place.

Through the years, while doing my research for my books and going to the boxing gyms, I had been in a couple of tight spots, and on one occasion, I found myself being surrounded by eleven enthusiastic gang members with one of them pressing a gun into the back of my head, saying, "Let's blow this mutherfucker's head off".

Fate was kind that day, but I didn't fancy my chances a second time around, so I thanked the girl for the advice. The girl said she could organise an "Uber but not an Uber" and I said, "Brilliant!". It was a small win for me as I booked my ride for a 6:30 am pick up the next morning.

The drive was eight minutes by car and when we arrived, it was us and three cats. We left at 7:30am and returned at 9:30, and this time, the door was open. I asked the lady to wait, and I walked into a pitch-black gym. There was an icy wind blowing and as I walked back to the car, a white minivan drove towards me and parked up. I recognised the driver. It was Mark Breland.

Breland was a five times New York Golden Gloves champion, and he had won the Gold medal at the 1984 Olympic games and when he turned professional, he became a world champion.

I walked to the van and greeted Breland. I had trained with him years ago in 'Gleasons Gym' in New York, but he couldn't remember me.

Breland was now working as part of Wilder's coaching team and he was brought in by Jay Deas, as an asset, with his calm demeanour and personality and his vast experience at the highest level.

I talked to Mark, explaining why I had travelled from Australia, and he shook his head in disbelief. I said goodbye to my ride and asked her if she could pick me up later that day.

I met the guys in the gym, and I asked if I could do a bit of training while I was waiting on Deas and Wilder.

The gym was getting busy, and there were young kids, amateur and professional boxers, getting ready to work out and spar, and there was older guys wrapped up in plastic, training to fight their middle age spread.

The gym was basic, with one ring, four heavy bags, one speed bag and a hydro uppercut bag all being battered and pounded and swinging back and forth in a squeaking, pendulum motion, with their chains creaking above in the rafters.

Sparring went on all afternoon and the fighters would come and go.

I was then told that Wilder wasn't coming as he was doing his swimming training today and I was told I had to come back tomorrow. I waited outside for my ride, but she never showed up. It was dark as I walked under the railway bridge.

That night I received a call from Deas, and I explained why I was in town. We had a great chat, and the ice had been broken.

The next morning, I went for a walk, and I talked to the local people. They told me that Tuscaloosa had bounced back after experiencing a mile wide tornado that devastated the area in 2011, killing sixty-five people and injuring fifteen hundred citizens. Other than the tragedy of lost lives, the financial cost was close to three billion dollars. Since that time, the city has come back with industry such as their Mercedes Benz factory and a large steel mill, plus the revenue that was generated by their college football team.

They also told me that Wilder was very popular in Tuscaloosa after growing up there, living there and he not only gave back to his hometown community but also to the disadvantaged areas of the surrounding towns. He was so well thought of that there was plans to erect a statue of him along 'The Black Warrior' river walk.

After my walk and meeting the local people, I organised my ride to the gym. When the lady turned up, there was a baby in the back and a small dog that was having a bad hair day. The baby was screaming, and the dog was barking but I knew I was only eight minutes away.

The lady driver asked me if I had met Deontay yet. I said, "No". She asked me if I had met a lot of boxers, and I told her I had. She then asked me if I had met Rocky, and I spent the last couple of minutes of the journey, telling her that Rocky was just a movie.

I got inside the gym and waited until Wilder and his three sparring partners arrived. When they arrived, it was all business. Their hands wrapped and shadow boxing, as they warmed up. I had been in many world champions training camps through the years, and on occasions, it had been chaos, with so many people and hangers-on, that there was barely room to move. Tonight, it felt right. Wilder's team was small, but they all had their job to do and every one of them were there for Wilder.

Wilder lay down in the ring and Joey Scott began to contort and twist and stretch Wilder into impossible positions until he submitted to the pain.

Wilder jumped up and screamed and that was the signal for the sparring to start. Each sparring partner did four hard rounds. After the twelve rounds, Wilder hit the bag briefly then he had some physio on his ankle then he had a full body massage.

After training, we went for dinner and we talked about boxing and the sacrifices the boxers had made, being away from their families, while trying to give them a better life.

The next day, we went to a fitness centre and Wilder worked out on his cardio and strength training. I have never seen a heavyweight train as long and as hard as Wilder.

He trained like a world class athlete, and everything was planned and done correctly.

After training, Jay Deas asked me if I would like to join them on a trip to one of the areas where Wilder helps out and contributes funds for the disadvantaged youth. The locals had told me, and I wanted to see for myself.

When we arrived, there was ten kids exercising and playing on the gym mats in a community centre building that Wilder pays for. They were having fun and laughing, and it was great to see.

When it was time to go, I noticed the kids were all putting their shoes on and some were badly in need of repair, and some had two different shoes on, but one kid stood out to me. He was wearing men's cowboy boots that were way too big for him. It broke my heart to see this, so I pulled out my wallet, and Deas grabbed my hand and said, "Please no, don't give them money. I thank you from my heart but if you give them money, their mom and dad will take it and spend it on drugs."

We walked out and went to a shop that was like a shack with iron bars on the windows and doors. As we walked inside, Deas said to me, "We bring the kids here and every time, the same thing happens. Watch! When you were a kid and you were asked what you wanted to buy in a shop, you would pick a candy bar, right? Watch these kids." Deas said to them, "Go and pick something!"

The kids all ran and came back with cans of food. I was emotional and I had tears rolling down my face.

The next day, I bought each kid a pair of sneakers. For me, it was a small thing to do but nothing compared to the ongoing commitment from Deontay Wilder. He was a son of Tuscaloosa and an inspiration to many, and it was a privilege to see the beauty in the beast.

Wilder won his first 32 fights by knockout to then fight the 239 lb (108 kilo) Haiti-born WBC champion, Bermane Stiverne in 2015.

Stiverne had knocked out Chris Arreola in the sixth round for the vacant WBC belt in 2014 in Los Angeles.

Going into the fight, he had twenty-one knockouts in twenty-five fights. In the fight, the heavier champion was kept at bay by Wilder's punishing hard jab, and he took some big right hands along the way. The man known as 'The Bronze Bomber' was too good, winning by a unanimous points victory in Las Vegas, to become the heavyweight champion of the world.

From there, he blitzed his next five opponents with his wild punching style. He was a dangerous man.

In late 2017, Wilder fought Stiverne in the rematch. Stiverne came in heavy. He hadn't fought for two years, and he paid the price for it. Wilder came out like a man possessed, beating his chest, to then unleash a bomb on the man from Haiti that sent him down like a wet suit to the floor.

Stiverne rose up but he was all but done. Wilder hammered him, dropping him again until his body and soul was crushed in the first round.

In his fortieth fight, Wilder defended his title for the tenth time against the undefeated Cuban Southpaw, Luis 'King Kong' Ortiz.

In the fight, the experienced cagey veteran was out-boxing Wilder, and he was winning the fight. Wilder was desperately looking for the big right hand, which came hard and fast in the fifth round, and again in the tenth round, with Ortiz going down twice before the fight was stopped in New York, with Wilder winning in devastating fashion.

It was now 2018, and Tyson Fury was back from oblivion, after retiring into a world of madness, binge drinking, and depression in 2015. He came back after two and a half years away from boxing and fought his way into heavyweight contention for Wilder's heavyweight crown.

In the fight, Fury feinted and jabbed his way through the rounds, catching Wilder with a few hard right hands. Wilder was using his jab but always looking for the big right hand. It was a close fight until the ninth round when Wilder threw a combination that sent Fury down. The English Gypsy got up and came back with a flurry to end the 10 points to 8 round.

The tenth round was closely fought, and the eleventh saw Fury feinting and jabbing while Wilder was looking for the big finisher. In the final round, Wilder hit Fury with a left hook that stunned Fury to then land another left hook, followed by a big right hand that hurt Fury with Wilder catching him again with a left hook that sent Fury down hard. The back of Fury's head slammed against the canvas, and he lay there staring at the rafters, while the referee began to count the knockdown. Unbelievably, Fury got up to beat the count and recovered enough to hold and throw, maul and grab to survive the final round. With Fury down twice and two 10 points to 8 rounds against him in the fight, the scorecards were read out. The judges scored 115-111 to Wilder. 114-110 to Fury and 113-113. The fight was ruled as a split decision, draw in the 'City of Angels'.

My thoughts are, if the fight was staged in New York, Fury would have been counted out and wilder would have won. Fury showed unbelievable will and courage, but he was fortunate to get a 114–110 score from one judge. That was the defining factor in the fight being ruled a draw.

Wilder came back five months later and destroyed Dominic Breazeale, to then go on to a rematch with Ortiz. In the fight, Wilder again, started slow, but he eventually took out the ageing Cuban in the seventh round.

Wilder then fought Fury in a rematch in Las Vegas and in the fight, Fury clubbed and mauled Wilder around the ring from the opening bell. Wilder had blood coming from his ear, and he was absolutely shell shocked with his eyes glazed over. Fury dominated the seven rounds until the towel was thrown into the ring to end the mauling. Wilder took a lot of damage in the fight and his corner saved him from serious injury.

The two would meet for a trilogy fight in Las Vegas, which was billed as 'Once and for All' and it was a battle for the ages.

In the fight, Wilder fought with a huge heart, being mauled and battered by Fury's one two punches. Fury was knocked down twice in the fourth round, surviving once again, and getting up after the bell. It was a back-and-forth slugfest that turned into a battle of attrition, with both fighters fighting on instinct. In the end, the mauling style from Fury had Wilder exhausted and 'The Gypsy King' knocked him down in the tenth and eleventh round to win by knockout in a modern-day heavyweight classic.

Wilder returned one year later in his forty sixth fight, to violently knockout his former sparring partner, Robert Helenius in the first round. There was talk of retirement, of life after boxing and spending precious time with his family but Wilder came back again after fourteen months away, to fight the New Zealand Samoan, puncher, Joseph Parker in Saudi Arabia.

In the fight, Parker took the fight to Wilder, throwing wild hooks to catch Wilder off balance and unsettling him enough to stop Wilder from getting into the fight and he fought a tremendous tactical fight to win on points.

When I watched the fight, I reflected on Wilder's brutal fights with Fury, and I thought about how much damage he had taken, and I hoped he would retire and enjoy his life.

Wilder had other ideas, and he came back once again in early June 2024 to face the plodding but powerful puncher, Zhilei Zhang in the desert of Saudi. Zhang was a silver medallist in the 2008 Olympics, and he was a clubbing, thudding southpaw from China with twenty-six wins and twenty-one knockouts.

At the weigh in, the 282-pound (127 kilos) Zhang outweighed Wilder by close to *70 pounds* (31 kilos).

In the fight, Wilder was hesitant to throw anything meaningful, while Zhang was trying to find his range early on. Zhang was throwing slow right-hand jabs and Wilder was parrying his shots while trying to load up his own big right hand. Wilder started to throw meaningful punches in the fourth round that seemed to wake up Zhang to end the round.

In the fifth round, with Wilder looking to land his own right hand, Zhang connected with his in a split-second counter punch right hook that had Wilder spinning around and stunned, and leaving himself wide open, the man known as 'Big Bang' knocked Wilder down with another right hook. Wilder bravely rose to his feet to fight on, but the referee had seen enough and stopped the fight. It was over.

Wilder will always be remembered for his trilogy with Fury, but he should also be remembered for his sixteen-year, 48-fight career as a wild throwing knockout machine that brought excitement to the heavyweight division.

He will be remembered as a man for the people of Alabama and a son of Tuscaloosa.

CAREER TOTALS

As of mid-2025, Wilder's fight record was 43 wins (42 KOs), 4 losses (3 KOs) and 1 draw.

What time did you get up in the morning?

I get up around 7:00 am.

Do you run in the morning?

Occasionally I do. I don't run long distances. I run on a treadmill at a good pace for endurance and I run on the sand, and I run through the woods. It's good to mix it up.

Do you stretch your body?

Yes. Stretching is a big part of training for me. I stretch every muscle in this body. It's intense.

What do you eat for breakfast?

I burn a lot in training, so I need to eat. I eat everything but I like sausage, pancakes, eggs, some toast, juice, and I drink protein shakes.

What do you do after breakfast?

I relax, and I look at my day and my business. I never stop. I also eat every couple of hours in between workouts. I'll eat good food like chicken, fish, tuna on a sandwich. High protein.

How many days are you in the gym?

I work out every day. I do gym workouts, cardio, strength and I do my boxing, and I love being in the pool. It varies but it all gets done. It also depends on how my body feels and where we are in training camp.

What time do you do your boxing workout?

I get there around 5:30 pm. If it's sparring, around 6:00 pm. I prepare mentally before I get there and while I am being stretched out, and while I'm moving around the ring. I train for 2 hours, and I finish around 8:00 pm.

What is your favourite exercise in the gym?

I enjoy practicing my punches on the mitts. Everything has to be done to be the best. I enjoy sparring in camp.

What do you eat for Dinner?

I like steak, chicken, everything. I have corn, yams, mashed potatoes, beans. Protein shake and water and some juice.

What do you do for fun or a hobby?

I have many things I like doing. I love music. I have a studio where I go and make music. I like being in the water, so I do scuba diving. It's beautiful and it's just you in there. I like nice things, and I love cars. My favourite thing is taking my wife and family on holidays we would never have dreamed of. I also like giving back to the people.

Did you have a job?

I had a few jobs. When I started boxing, I received sponsorship from a local businessman who helped me. I worked as a delivery driver for Budweiser. I unloaded 100s of boxes of beer every day and I treated it like training. I enjoyed it.

What time do you go to sleep?

Around 11:00 pm.

NON-SPARRING DAYS

5-day workout

Monday

- Gym work – Drills for agility.
- Stretching full body 20 minutes.
- Short sharp controlled sprints which is similar to soccer player drills. Running short distance around cones and ladder at fast pace. Knees up alternating as he moves forward.
- Core work / stomach and lower back exercises – sit ups, leg raises.
- 250 total.

Tuesday

- Aquatic training in pool.
- Low impact effective resistance on Wilder's body.
- Alternating leg split jumps.
- Squats.
- Jogging stationary.
- Running motion through the water.
- Shadow Boxing.
- Leg jumps from one leg to the other as he moved up the pool.
- Swim 10 laps of 25 metre pool.

Wednesday

- Stretching.
- Massage.
- Rest and recover.
- Aches and pain therapy.

Thursday

- Gym work for Strength and agility 90 minutes.
- Stretching full body 20 minutes.
- Leg Hops.
- Calf Raises.
- Leg press.
- Deadlift.
- Squats.
- Lunges.
- Leg hops.
- Agility drills around cones and ladders.

Friday

- Stretching full body.
- Strength workout.
- Squat jumps.
- Lifting knees up high alternating while moving forward.
- Leg Hops.
- Lunges.
- Light weight – explosive working arms, shoulders back and chest.

SPARRING DAYS

- 6:00 pm to 8:00 pm.
- 2-hour session.
- Sparring is twice per week.
- 3 Sparring Partners waiting.
- Wrap / Tape Hands.
- Full body stretching by Wilder and his conditioning coach.

Note: I have never seen any boxer who stretches so intensely. Every part of his body was stretched and manipulated, bending and pulling him like he was made of rubber for 35 minutes.

- Shadow Box 3 rounds x 3 minutes with a 1-minute break in between each round.
- Focus mitts 3 rounds x 3 minutes with a 1-minute break.
- Sparring begins.
- Depending on the stage of training camp. 6 rounds x 3 minutes with a 1-minute break in between each round. This progresses to 8 rounds then 10 to reach the championship rounds of 12 rounds. Note: When I was there, Wilder did 12 hard rounds with 3 Sparring partners on rotation of 2 rounds.
- Gloves off.
- Warm down / Moving around in circles around the ring while loosening up. 5 minutes.
- Hand Wraps off.
- Wilder leaves the ring and lies down on massage table. 5-minute light massage to finish.

MARVELOUS MARVIN HAGLER

'Destruction and Destroy'

BIOGRAPHY

Marvin Hagler was born on the 23rd of May 1954, in one of the poorest neighbourhoods in Newark, New Jersey. He was born in tough times, and he lived in a rundown tenement with his brother Robbie Sims, and his mother, Ida Mae Hagler who also had four daughters to care for.

Ida Mae was living on welfare, struggling and doing whatever she could to feed and raise her family. In 1967, there was unrest and violence in the streets of Newark, where horrific urban race riots had broken out all around them.

For five dark days, there was relentless armed conflict, arson, looting, and beatings in the streets and alleyways, with twenty-six people losing their lives and hundreds left badly injured.

The bitter social unrest wasn't over, and the streets continued to boil over until 1969 where more chaos and violence erupted.

In desperation Ida Mae Haglar gathered whatever they had and took her children and left Newark and moved to Boston Massachusetts, hoping for a better life.

As a young boy, Marvin walked up the long wooden stairs to the gym and introduced himself to brothers Pat and Goody Petronelli, telling them he wanted to be a boxer.

Through time, the two Italian World War Two veterans built what they called 'a triangle of trust' with the young Hagler and while one managed, the other trained him.

In 1973, the nineteen-year-old won the USA National amateur middleweight title and a few weeks later he turned professional.

Fighting often, Hagler's road was always going to be a hard road, with no Olympic accolades, big money promoters or money makers backing him, Hagler had hunger inside, the will to win, the belief in himself and the desire to become the middleweight champion of the world.

In 1974, he fought eleven times facing the 1972 Olympic gold medallist, Sugar Ray Seales twice, beating him on points and then settling for a draw in the rematch. From there, he fought with some of the toughest, most avoided fighters in the middleweight division, travelling to fight in their backyards. In 1976, he went to Philadelphia to face Bobby 'Boogaloo' Watts and was beaten on a close majority decision. Two months later, he was beaten again in 'The City Of Brotherly Love' by the fast moving, hard man, Willie 'The Worm' Monroe. Monroe beat Hagler on points, bursting a blood vessel in Hagler's nose and giving him a lesson he never forgot.

Hagler went back to Brockton and trained harder than ever before. After stopping the dangerous Eugene Hart, he went on to knock out Willie Monroe twice in 1977, in impressive, performances of controlled aggression and pressure, leaving no doubt he was ready for *anyone*.

I was lucky to meet Marvin Hagler twice. The first time was a strange experience for a couple of reasons that I'll explain later. The second time I talked to Hagler in New York, we talked for hours about his fights, his training and his mindset and drive to be the best. Hagler said, "I worked very hard and all I did was practice and think about being the middleweight champion of the world. I worked all day in construction for four dollars an hour and I trained for two hours every day and ran every morning before work. I fought anyone and that's what you need to do to be champion."

It was now 1978 and Hagler fought five times, battering the Englishman Kevin Finnegan in two bloody fights, leaving the Cockney with multiple gashes to his eyes and cheekbone.

Next up was the dangerous veteran 'Bad' Bennie Briscoe. Briscoe had been fighting for years, and he had travelled around the world fighting Vito Antuofermo, Emile Griffith, Eugene Hart, Eddie Mustafa Muhammad, Tony Mundine, Rodrigo Valdez and Carlos Monzon. A sanitation worker by day, chasing and battering rats with a baseball bat to then go to his gym in Philadelphia and batter sparring partners until it was time to go home. In their fight, Hagler boxed brilliantly, maintaining control with his southpaw jab and vicious body attacks that eventually broke down the hard man, Briscoe, beating him on points in Philadelphia. After making short work of Sugar Ray Seales, destroying him in the first round, Hagler in his fiftieth fight, finally got his chance to fight for the middleweight championship of the world. His opponent was the Italian champion Vito Antuofermo.

Antuofermo had been working as a meat cutter in New York trying to live, before he travelled to Monte Carlo in the French Riviera in June 1979 to challenge the Argentinian champion, Hugo Corro, battering him to the head and body in a fight he won by a very close split decision. Corro had been fighting since 1971 and he had shared the ring with Emile Griffith, Bennie Briscoe and Eugene Hart and he was tough and very durable but due to his style of fighting, he was prone to getting cut badly around his eyes.

In the fight, Hagler went to work on the Italian early, jabbing, and hooking, leaving the champion taking and absorbing punishment. The proud Antuofermo came back strong in the middle rounds but in the end Hagler was more accurate, and his punches were more effective, hurting and pushing Antuofermo back with his fast combinations until the bell rang. After fifteen rounds, the fight was declared a controversial split decision draw. Hagler had been denied.

Vito Antuofermo returned to Las Vegas a few months later, losing in a close fight to Alan Minter and although Minter was down in the fourteenth round, the ringside judges scored it a split decision to the English fighter. Three months later, Antuofermo travelled to London to have another go, but this time, Minter made no mistake, dominating and punching his way, jabbing and peppering Antuofermo's face until he bled, and bled until the fight was stopped in the eighth round in front of Minter's adoring fans at Wembley.

After the disappointment in Las Vegas, Hagler moved on, and after knocking out Bobby Watts in the second round, and settling the score, he could not be denied.

In September 1980, he crossed the pond and challenged Antuofermo-conqueror Alan Minter for the Undisputed middleweight championship of the world. The build up to the fight was marred by ugly racial tensions, by Minter's English fans. Minter added fuel to the already roaring fire, saying, "I've worked too hard to lose my title to a black man."

Hagler harnessed his anger inside until the bell rang then he unleashed his assault on Minter, out classing and busting up the Londoner to snatch his titles, after picking off Minter at will in the third round to become the Undisputed Champion of the world. It was a brutal, spiteful and dominating performance but after riots broke out from hooligans, and beer bottles and cans being launched into the crowd and the ring, Hagler had to get out of there and wait until he got home to Brockton to celebrate his victory.

Hagler took some time out to rest and enjoy what he had worked and toiled so hard for but two months later, he was back at Cape Cod training harder with the mindset of a challenger, not a champion. When I asked him what it felt like to be the only undisputed champion in the world at that time in boxing, he said, "I worked too hard to get soft. There was no easy way for me. I worked and worked, and I never ducked anyone. I ran in the cold, and I put myself in jail and I did the work as that's what had to be done."

Hagler made his first defence in Boston beating up the Venezuelan, Fulgencio Obelmejias in eight one sided rounds to then face Vito Antuofermo in a rematch. Antuofermo had been in the wars with Minter in a contest that was stopped in the eighth round due to cuts.

Antuofermo was like a rotten tooth that needed pulling out, and Hagler wanted to set the record straight. Antuofermo fancied his chances, with both men looking chiselled and appearing to be made from rock. In the fight, Hagler was too fast and accurate and after head clashes from Antuofermo, burrowing in wildly, fighting and doing what he could to unsettle Hagler. Antuofermo's head burst open, and, in the end, and full of blood, after a reign of uppercuts and hooks, the proud Antuofermo stood on his feet at the end of the fourth round and didn't go out for the fifth round. He had taken enough. Antuofermo said goodbye to boxing but returned thirty-nine months later to then retire for good in 1985.

It was now Hagler's fifty-seventh fight. His next opponent was the tough, come forward fighter from Syria, Mustafa Hamsho, who had come to New York as a stow away when he was a young man. He was unbeaten in twenty-seven fights, and he was fearless, powerful and he could punch. Hagler out boxed the tough New York strong man taking everything out of him, ripping open his face with fast combination punching that forced 'the Syrian Buzzsaw' to be saved by his corner in the eleventh round.

It seemed that there was a never-ending line up of challengers, waiting, and wanting what Hagler had. Next up was the big punching fighter from Philadelphia, Bill 'Caveman' Lee. He was a renowned puncher that trained at the Kronk gym in Detroit, sparring anyone, anytime, Lee was always ready to fight, and he took the fight at just two weeks' notice. It was seen by many as a tough fight, but Hagler destroyed him in sixty-seven seconds, hitting him with a right hook that sent him back to the Stone Age. Lee left the sport for four years, got hooked on cocaine, and was incarcerated for armed robbery, spending a total of sixteen years inside.

Hagler was relentless and hungrier than ever in his training, and preparation to not just win but to defend what was his. After travelling to San Remo, Italy to beat Fulgencio Obelmejias in the fifth round, Hagler returned home to Boston to defend his title for the sixth time against the Englishman, Tony Sibson.

Sibson was a proud strong fighting man, and he was very popular due to his exciting come forward aggressive style. He won the Commonwealth and European title, stopping Alan Minter in the third round at Wembley and he earned the right to face Hagler after fifty-one fights as a professional.

Hagler was relentless and battered Sibson to the head and body, switching from southpaw to orthodox, finally hammering him to the canvas in the sixth round. If anyone was looking for any chinks in Hagler that night, or any signs of decline, or even doubting his desire to keep fighting, this fight had Hagler at his most calculated, meanest, and ferocious best, arguably fighting at his peak after sixty fights.

Brockton heavyweight champion, Rocky Marciano fought forty-nine fights and was undefeated. He could have fought on, but he decided to walk away. 'The Brown Bomber' Joe Louis could have walked away but he kept fighting. He fought everyone in a long seventeen-year career, fighting in 69 fights and in his final fight, he was knocked down twice and sent through the ropes by a punch from Marciano.

Hagler had heard the stories and had been fighting long enough to know when he would walk away. Joe Louis famously said, "It's hard to get up and run when you are wearing silk pyjamas."

It was now 1983 and after Hagler took care of business and took out Wilford Scypion in brutal fashion in the fourth round, all the talk had been about him fighting the Panamanian wild man, Roberto 'Hands of Stone' Duran.

At this stage of his life in boxing, Duran was the challenge Hagler needed.

Duran had been fighting all his life, born into poverty in the slums of El Chorrillo in Panama in 1951. He started boxing at eight years old and he was regarded as one of the greatest lightweights, dominating the division with his ferocious style of fighting.

Going into the Hagler fight, after years of living the high life, boiling down to make the weight, and living with the highs of winning and also living with the lowest of lows in defeat and humiliation, it seemed boxing had beaten Duran down. Just as Hagler needed Duran, it was Duran who needed Hagler. Without him, it was over.

Hagler went into camp and trained like a man possessed, battering his sparring partners, shouting and snarling at them, saying, "C'mon fight! Fight!", and after training he retreated to the solitary of his room. Pat Petronelli famously said, "As the fight approaches, he goes to bed earlier every night. He's such poor company and becomes so unpleasant ... that he likes to get to bed early to cut down on the time he has to spend with himself".

Duran promised that he would train hard, and he did – running, sparring, jumping rope, and staying off the Coca Cola.

When they both weighed in, Hagler was 157.5 pounds (71.4 kilos), and Duran came in at 156.5 (70.9 kilos).

The fight was scheduled for fifteen rounds, but many thought it wouldn't go the distance.

They were wrong.

They underestimated the man from Panama, who had all those years of fighting experience under his belt, who had wins over many world champions, and who still had the self-belief to win.

In the fight, Hagler was bigger and stronger, but Duran used every bit of his eighty-two-fight experience to duck and weave, bobbing and counter punching Hagler to frustrate the champion from Brockton. Hagler used his jab to great effect and poured on a two-fisted attack that pressured Duran, forcing him backwards. Duran came back courageously but he tired, and Hagler went to work, hammering Duran until the final bell. It was a great performance by Duran, but Hagler fought brilliantly, closing the show and leaving no doubt he was the best middleweight in the world.

Duran fought on in huge fights, winning and losing to come back, time after time, to become a legend in the history books of boxing.

Hagler fought twice in 1984. First up was the Argentinian 'Hammer' Juan Roldan, who had been fighting on Hagler's undercards. He was aggressive and strong, and he could punch. He earned his shot at Hagler after icing the southpaw, Frank 'The Animal' Fletcher with a big right hand that knocked him through the ropes in the sixth round at Caesars Palace.

Roldan was tough and he fought with courage after taking heavy damage to his right eye, with Hagler opening up on him with slashing hooks, switching from southpaw, and catching the brave challenger with a big right-hand punch that put him down. The Argentinian put his head down. He had enough.

In October, Hagler destroyed Mustafa Hamsho with an onslaught of brutal punches, knocking him down hard in the third round in the tenth defence of his title.

Tommy Hearns had been boxing since he was nine years old, campaigning in 163 contests in the amateurs. He turned professional in 1977 under the watchful eye of Emanuel Steward at the Kronk Gym in Detroit. At 6'1 he was very tall with long arms, and he would eventually use his natural abilities of lateral movement and sheer hard work, turning him into a fast and devastating puncher at welterweight. Going into the fight with Hagler, Hearns had only been beaten once in forty-one fights by Sugar Ray Leonard and in his most recent fight, he knocked out Roberto Duran cold in the second round. With thirty-two knockouts, he was a dangerous man.

The build up to the fight, scheduled for twelve rounds was unbelievable. Stubborn egos and genuine dislike for each other, with neither man giving an inch.

The fight was billed as 'The War' and Hagler and Hearns trained harder than ever before. Sparring partners would come and go after being brutalised by both Hearns and Hagler. There was a lot of media and TV interviews and while Hagler was a good talker, knowing what to say and when to say it, Hearns wasn't. Emanuel Steward brought in former entertainment writer, and First Lady of Boxing, Jackie Kallen, to assist with coaching Hearns on how to talk and what to say when being interviewed in front of the camera. Hearns was a street kid with little education and Kallen taught him simple things like pausing before answering and reminding him to say 'Well, basically' at the beginning of each question he had to answer to buy him some time to think. She taught him to be calm and smile and for him to stop saying 'man' all the time and to avoid using profanities. I asked Jackie Kallen if this was correct, and she confirmed this to be true.

Expectations were high and in the fight, Hagler and Hearns rushed out of their corners and went to war with no regard for their own safety, clashing in the centre of the ring, they each unloaded wild hooks and punches with such ferocity, leaving Hearns damaged, breaking his right hand on Hagler's head. Hagler sustained a bad cut, and he had blood pouring down his face. It was mayhem. In round two, both champions looking deranged, threw everything they had with intense bad intentions. Something had to give and in the third round, Hagler stalked Hearns desperately trying to get in under his long powerful jab, while blood running down his face and in real danger of the fight being stopped, Hagler lunged in, catching Hearns with a right hook that sent Hearns in a backward motion to the ropes, and his legs betraying him, finally collapsing to the canvas, lying flat on his back. It was brutal and it was over.

The man known as the 'Motor City Cobra' fought on until 2006, retiring after a 67-fight career spanning almost three decades, and becoming a world champion in five different weight divisions.

John Mugabi was born in Uganda in 1960. He started boxing as a young boy and he had a long and successful amateur career, with 195 fights, representing Uganda at the 1980 Olympic Games in Moscow.

He moved to London and turned professional at the end of 1980.

He was a strong fearsome puncher, and he had won his first twenty-five fights by breaking down his opponents with his fierce attack and brutal finishing, earning him the nickname, 'The Beast'.

Mugabi was the number one contender, and he was next in line to face Hagler in his twelfth defence.

Hagler took on the challenge with vigour, dismissing the twenty-six-year-old knockout artist as just another opponent, saying he would 'feast on the beast'.

Although he was the betting favourite, all eyes were on Hagler to see if he could take the pressure and the power punches from Mugabi. In the fight, Hagler used his southpaw jab to pressure and dictate the pace of the fight, doubling and trebling up with hard left hooks, and going to Mugabi's body to take his legs away. Mugabi was as hard as they come but the pace of the fight and the body punches had him exhausted, and Hagler battered Mugabi with two right hands which took the African Lion's heart, knocking him down in the eleventh round. Hagler was Marvelous.

John Mugabi would fight on, realising his dream of becoming a world champion, winning the WBC junior middleweight title in 1989. He retired in 1999.

After the Mugabi fight, Hagler's star was shining brightly, and he went on vacation, and he enjoyed himself doing commercials and appearing on late night TV. Life was good. He wasn't at the stage that he was wearing silk pyjamas just yet. There was talk of Carlos Monzon's seven-year undefeated run and his world championship record of fourteen defences in his reign as champion in the 1970s, and there was a lot of talk about a rematch with Tommy Hearns. There was a lot of talk about Hagler retiring. Hagler didn't think Hearns deserved a second fight and he brushed off questions of retirement, saying, "I will know when it's time. I will retire in peace".

Sugar Ray Leonard's name was back in the conversation again, irritating Hagler, opening a sore that he had been itching since 1982.

After months of talk and negotiations, it was announced that Leonard would be returning to face Hagler in April 1987.

Leonard was as charismatic as he was intelligent. He had won the Gold medal at the 1976 Olympic games in Montreal, becoming an American Hero. He turned professional in 1977 after a tremendous amateur career of 165 wins with 75 stoppages and 5 losses.

Leonard was a promoter's dream with a smile that could light up a dark room on a cloudy day, but as soon as he wrapped his hands and put the gloves on, he transformed into a beast. He had lightning speed with fast hands, and the ability to move his feet effortlessly in and out while having the balance and skill to fire off stinging accurate combination punches that made him a multiple-world-champion and a boxing superstar.

Going into his super fight with Hagler, Leonard wanted three items of note, added into the rules of engagement, which were:

1. The size of the ring had to be larger at twenty feet square;
2. The size of the gloves had to be bigger at 10 ounces, and have the thumb stitched to the glove; and
3. The fight could only be fought over twelve rounds.

Hagler agreed and was compensated for his troubles. Leonard was coming back from a three-year break from boxing, having retired in 1982 and then again in 1984 due to a detached retina to his right eye. It was also well documented that Leonard had never fought at 160 pounds, but behind the scenes, he had been busy, fighting strong middleweight contenders in heavy sparring in preparation for Hagler.

Hagler was highly motivated and driven for this fight. It had been a long road, and he had fought them all, had defended his title twelve times and was undefeated in seven years.

Only Leonard remained. Hagler expected a hard fight, and he trained in solitude in Palm Springs.

When the bell rang for the first round, after years of talking, the whole world stopped and watched in anticipation and excitement. In the fight Leonard used the ring, dancing and catching Hagler with fast flurries, but also hitting Hagler low and holding. Hagler stalked Leonard and pressured him to go backwards to the ropes and he also connected with the stronger punches, hurting Leonard in the fifth round and the ninth. With Leonard tiring after the pace of the fight and the body punches he had taken, it seemed Hagler had him, then unbelievably, he would come back with fast eye-catching combinations. Hagler had also tired but continued to throw punches. Going into the last round, Hagler cut off the ring and threw the more telling blows, finishing strongly.

After a tremendous fight, the judges scores were read out to the sold-out crowd in Las Vegas. 115–113 to Leonard. 115–113 for Hagler and unbelievably 118–110 for Leonard. Leonard won by a split decision.

I remember watching the fight like it was yesterday.

I thought Hagler won all those years ago and all these years later, I *still* think he won.

Sugar Ray Leonard fought on beating Donny Lalonde on points, and drawing with Tommy Hearns and he beat Roberto Duran on points, before retiring again in 1989. He came back in 1991 to fight for the junior middleweight championship against Terry

MARVELOUS MARVIN HAGLER

Norris, being beaten down and knocked down in rounds two and seven to lose on points. Unbelievably, Leonard returned for the last time in 1997 at the age of forty, to challenge Hector Camacho but he was stopped in the fifth round. It was time to say 'Goodbye'.

Hagler never returned to fight again. He knew it was time to get out. He announced his retirement from boxing after watching his brother Robbie Sims lose to the WBA middleweight champion, Sumbu Kalambay in June 1988.

I first met Hagler in New York. I was so determined and excited to have the opportunity to meet and talk with my boyhood hero. I introduced myself and we took photos, and we were talking about his fights and his training, and it was going brilliantly. Out of nowhere, a guy approached waving his arm and telling Hagler it was time to leave. Hagler said, "Vinnie, give us a few minutes then we'll go." At that point this guy tried pushing in past me to then say, "We need to go!" As he pushed, I said "Calm down. I'll be finished in a minute." Vinnie was getting angry with the situation as Hagler was now smiling and telling him to take it easy. Vinnie was now bursting at the seams, and he tried to push me, and I pushed back and for a split second, I had the terrible realisation that I could be trading punches with this guy with my favourite fighter of all time watching on. We stood there, his head on mine, and mine pushing on his, with Vinnie saying to me through gritted teeth, "If we go outside, I'll shoot you."

I replied, "You better be fucking quick. Now fuck off!"

To my pleasant surprise, Hagler's wife arrived and diffused the situation and Hagler shrugged his shoulders and laughed and told me it was great talking to me, and we shook hands again and Hagler walked and waved. I stood there thinking what had just happened and I left a happy man.

As a fighter, fighting at 160 pounds his whole career, the fighters he fought, and being undefeated for seven years, winning the undisputed middleweight championship of the world.

Marvelous Marvin Hagler was one of the greatest middleweights in the history of the sport of boxing.

Marvelous Marvin Hagler. 1954–2021

CAREER TOTALS

Hagler retired with a fight record of 62 wins (52 KOs), 3 losses (3 KOs) and 2 draws.

"MY THINKING WAS ALWAYS, ALWAYS THE SAME. WHEN I GOT TO THE RING, IT WAS HIM AND ME. IT WAS WAR. DESTRUCTION AND DESTROY. I ALWAYS HAD TO PROVE PEOPLE WRONG."

MARVELOUS
MARVIN HAGLER

MARVELOUS MARVIN HAGLER – A DAY IN THE LIFE

What time did you get up in the morning?

6:00 am every day.

Did you do your roadwork then?

I ran 6 miles at a good pace. I did my roadwork in the rain and the freezing wind, and I ran through the ice and snow. When it was warmer, I would do 8 miles. I trained like my heroes did. I ran in heavy ankle boots, and I would run along the sand dunes of Cape Cod. I would shadow box and think of who I was fighting. I would run going backwards for a mile or so and shadow box. I increased my speed as I got close to the end.

Did you stretch your body before you ran?

I did a light stretch. Nothing crazy.

What did you do after your run?

I would come back to the hotel, and I would take my boots off, and I would do sit ups at the fire. I washed up then I had some breakfast.

What did you have for breakfast?

I had cereal with milk. I had cornflakes and sugar pops mixed in. I had some fruit. I liked pears when they had them and I had grapefruit juice. I wanted to train to fight so in training, I had just enough food.

What did you do after breakfast?

I would go for a walk most of the time. I enjoyed my own company, and I did a lot of thinking. People got to know me there. I would go back to my room and rest. I tried to block out everything but sometimes I had to talk to reporters. I watched some TV, and I put on some music. I would read but mostly, I thought about the guy I was fighting and what I was going to do to him.

How many days did you train?

I trained every day. I trained for 2 hours. Hard. I've said it before, but I put myself here. It was the way it had to be. It was lonely but I liked the solitude. I liked being alone. Me and the seagulls. Nothing much to do.

What was your favourite exercise in the gym?

It all had to be done every day, but I liked refining my skills, practicing my punches with shadow boxing and using them in sparring. I liked hitting the speed bag.

What time did you finish in the gym?

It was usually around 6:00 pm until 8:30 pm every day. You never knew if you were sparring and neither did my sparring partners, but it was always 2 hours.

MARVELOUS MARVIN HAGLER – A DAY IN THE LIFE

What did you do after training?

I would go back to my room, wash up, and eat. Sometimes I would sit and look into the fire and think. I would read and make phone calls to my family. I had my food made for me and I liked chicken, vegetables, gravy. Healthy fresh food. I liked fish. I would eat just enough.

What did you do for fun or a hobby?

When I was training, I read and watched the TV. When the fight was over, I enjoyed spending time with my family. I enjoyed helping people where I could. I have always liked animals, and I collected pigeons.

Did you have a job?

Yes. I worked as a labourer in construction. When I was 14, I worked in a factory and later I worked in a leather factory. I always worked hard.

What time did you go to bed?

I watched TV until 9:00 pm, and I was sleeping by 10:00 pm.

MARVELOUS MARVIN HAGLER – THE WORKOUTS

NON-SPARRING DAYS

- Hand Wraps on / moving around.

Floor exercises – 300 of – always 3 minutes duration.

- Sit ups.
- Leg raises / hold while extended and raised 6 inches off the floor.
- Sit up with right elbow touching opposite left knee in a fast-twisting torso. Alternating, left elbow touching right knee.
- Leg raises / cross over. One foot over the other while raised and extended. Alternate cross overs.
- Sit ups with arms behind head to then bring knees up and touch knees with hands in one motion, focusing on squeezing the stomach together then arms back and legs back straight. Repeat.

Light Sparring begins-

- 1 Sparring Partner has warmed up and he is waiting to go. Another is warming up.
- Sparring partner is there to mimic opponent's style.
- 2 rounds x 3 minutes with a 1-minute break in between each round.
- Shadow Boxing while in the ring. 2 rounds x 3 minutes.
- Pad and Glove work – 4 rounds x 3 minutes with a 1-minute break in between each round. The trainer puts on a Focus mitt and glove and Hagler works on combination punches with 16-ounce gloves on and the trainer mimics his opponent as they move around the ring, bobbing and weaving while pushing him backwards.
- Heavy Bag 4 rounds x 3 minutes with a 1-minute break.
- Jump Rope 15 minutes non-stop.
- Speed Bag 3 rounds x 3 minutes.
- Shadow Boxing while looking in the mirror 3 rounds x 3 minutes.

FLOOR WORK – 10 minutes total

- Push ups.
- Pull ups.
- Side to sides.
- Torso standing twists.
- Touch toes stretch.
- Finish with 3 minutes skipping at medium pace.

SPARRING DAYS

- Wrap and tape hands.
- Floor exercises – 300 of. Everything is of 3-minutes duration.
- Sit ups.
- Leg raises – hold while raised and extended.
- Leg raises – cross over. One foot over the other and hold then alternate each foot and hold while raised 6 inches off the floor.
- Sit ups with arms behind head to then bring knees up and touch knees with hands in one motion, focusing on squeezing the stomach muscles and core together then arms back behind head and legs back straight. Repeat.
- Sit up with elbows touching opposite knees in a fast-twisting torso motion. Left elbow touching right knee and right elbow touching left knee, alternating.
- Jumping Rope 9 minutes non-stop.
- Shadow Boxing in the ring 3 rounds x 3 minutes with a 1-minute break each round.
- Sparring begins – Depending on training camp, there will be 4 to 6 Sparring partners waiting to go. Each boxer is on a 2-round rotation until the planned rounds are finished.
- Sparring 8 hard rounds x 3 minutes with a 1-minute break in between each round.
- Speed Bag 3 rounds x 3 minutes.
- Shadow Boxing in the mirror 3 rounds x 3 minutes.
- Finish with 3 minutes of skipping at a medium pace.

VITO ANTUOFERMO

'Invictus'

BIOGRAPHY

The sun was beating down on the back of the eight-year-old boy as he stumbled through the dreels of olive fields. Head down while blocking out the pain of blistered hands as the sweat nipped like acid, he focused on his only task which was to steer the stubborn beast and the wooden handles of the plough up the hill and back while it carved and gouged the sun-baked soil as they moved forward. The work was as hard as the land, and it was all he knew.

Vito Antuofermo was born in 1953 in a small town called Palo Del Colle which was situated close to the much bigger port city of Bari in the Apulia region of southern Italy.

Life was a tough hard slog, working the land, hoping for the seasons to be kind to them as the years went on, and praying for a good harvest. It was all they knew until the rain never came and the land died.

Antuofermo's mother and father made the difficult decision to splinter their family and leave their home to try to give their children a better chance to live. This new life was a million miles away in a strange land, and it was known as the home of the brave and the land of opportunity. Antuofermo stepped foot on American soil in 1969 and onto the tough streets of Brooklyn, New York, where he stayed with relatives. With no English, he walked the streets looking for a job, where he eventually found work, making sausage in the meat works. He would roam the streets, trying to find his way in his new world and trouble would often find him. In 1970, after being picked up by the police, one of the officers tried to talk to Antuofermo about channelling his aggression and fists, by learning how to box. He took the seventeen-year-old to the Police Athletic League gym in Flatbush, Brooklyn to see if something could be done to help him. Antuofermo worked hard in the gym, and he found somewhere to go and something to believe in. His new mentor and trainer, Joe La Guardia, told Vito stories about the Italian heavyweight great, Rocky Marciano to inspire him. Within months, he won the New York Golden Gloves as a welterweight novice. The following year, the 5'7 Italian brawler made it to the final of the Golden Gloves, where he faced the six-foot, Eddie Gregory. The height, size and reach of Gregory was too much in the contest and Antuofermo was beaten. Gregory turned professional and changed his name to Eddie Mustafa Muhammad and moved up in weight to win the WBA lightweight heavyweight world title in 1980.

After a 28 win-2 loss campaign as an amateur, Antuofermo decided not to take his chances of representing Italy or America in the 1972 Olympic Games in Munich and he turned professional in late 1971. Continuing to box, with the dream of becoming a world champion like Marciano wasn't going to be easy. Antuofermo had to find a comfortable weight to fight at as he knew he wasn't a big puncher in a world of killers. He knew he would need to train harder and try to wear down his opponents with his stamina and pressure punching style inside. He also had physical problems that could be detrimental as a fighter, with bad eyesight, a protruding bone structure, particularly around his eyes and he was born with a twisted right foot. When I interviewed Vito in New Jersey, he took his sneaker and his sock off to show me his foot. As I looked at his deformed twisted foot, I thought about how he had moved in the gym and in his fights and to say it was impossible to comprehend and see in my mind's eye, how he trained, sparred, skipped, plus all those years of roadwork, while preparing to fight.

Antuofermo was a born fighter, and he found a way to triumph over adversity.

Losing once to Harold Weston, in thirty-eight fights, the fight was stopped by the referee as Antuofermo was pummelling the former golden gloves champion on the ropes. Blood was pouring from a cut, and the ref had seen enough. After beating Dennis Moyer and Emile Griffith on points, it was now 1976 and Antuofermo travelled to Berlin, Germany to fight for the European Junior Middleweight title against the hometown favourite, Eckhard Dagge, beating him on points over fifteen rounds. He packed his bags and went back to Berlin, and he was beaten on points by Southpaw, Frank Wissenbach over 8 rounds. Later that year, Antuofermo travelled to Lazio, Italy to face Maurice Hope, for the European Junior Middleweight title, losing by a TKO in the fifteenth round. Hope hit Antuofermo with a fast Left right combination which connected to the back of his ear, which stunned, hurt and wobbled him which lead the referee to step in with only 12 seconds to go in the fight. He returned to New York and beat the big punching Eugene Hart in the fifth round in Philadelphia after taking heavy shots, to then slugging it out and beating the veteran hard man, Bennie Briscoe on points at 'The Garden'.

With these wins, and after 48 fights behind him, Antuofermo earned a shot at the world champion from Argentina, Hugo Pastor Corro. At stake was the undisputed middleweight championship of the world. The fight was held in Monte Carlo in June 1979.

In the fight, Antuofermo knew he couldn't out box the champion, so he had to be on him, fighting inside and he knew he had to throw a lot of punches to mitigate Corro's speed to win. Antuofermo did so, beating the Argentinian by a split decision over 15 rounds to become the undisputed middleweight champion of the world.

With little time to enjoy his win, Antuofermo was back in the gym, preparing to face the mean and hungry Southpaw, Marvelous Marvin Hagler. Hagler had been fighting since 1973, and he had earned the right to challenge for the belts. The fight was held at Caesars Palace in Las Vegas.

In the fight, Antuofermo brawled and battled his way through the fight, never taking a backward step but taking a lot of punches in the fight, with Hagler unable to hit him cleanly to knock him out. Antuofermo kept coming forward throwing punches, which frustrated Hagler to distraction, forcing the fight to go to the judges' scorecards. After fifteen hard rounds, the judges scored it a draw which was seen as a controversial decision by many. A jubilant Antuofermo was full of blood, as he left the arena receiving 74 stitches in his face after his first defence as the undisputed champion.

It was now early 1980 and with little time for healing to the scar tissue on his face, Antuofermo's next challenger was the tough and skilful London southpaw, Alan Minter. The Englishman was a bronze medallist in the 1972 Olympic Games in Munich and he had won the British and European titles since turning professional in 1972.

In the fight, Antuofermo fought the only way he knew, while Minter used the right-hand jab followed by a straight left. It was a gruelling fight with Minter boxing and winning the first few rounds until Antuofermo bulled his way back into the fight, winning the middle rounds. Minter was reliant on using the 1–2 but the champion was pressing the pace with his aggressive style. With both fighters cut over the eye from the twelfth round, Antuofermo was countering the English challenger with great success, knocking him down in the 14th round. The fight was close, going the distance. The English judge at ringside scored the fight wide in Minter's favour and he won by a split decision in Vegas. A little over three months later and Antuofermo travelled to London to face Minter in the rematch. Antuofermo trained in Italy for the fight, and he was also going to London without his long time cut man, Freddie Brown.

In the fight, Minter boxed brilliantly using his jab to great effect. Antuofermo's skin opened up in the first round as he tried to get inside. Minter's timing and counterpunching was the key to victory, and he beat Antuofermo to the punch the whole fight, until the corner stopped the fight in between the 8th and 9th round to retain his undisputed crown.

Antuofermo went home to Brooklyn for a well-deserved rest. Minter faced Marvelous Marvin Hagler three months later and was out boxed and battered in front of thousands of English fans at Wembley.

It was now 1981. Antuofermo had come back after surgery on his eyes, beating Mauricio Aldana on points in Chicago. Hagler was the undisputed middleweight champion of the world and yet he still had that itch to scratch which was Vito Antuofermo. The rematch was signed for June, and it was going to be a homecoming for the champion. In the fight, the unbeaten Hagler was boxing while Antuofermo was mauling his way inside with little success. He was fighting wild and angry, and after only 45 seconds of the first round, Antuofermo lunged in, banging his head with Hagler and a deep cut was opened. Freddie Brown was doing what he could, but the coagulant of Vaseline and adrenaline wasn't enough. With blood everywhere, Hagler was hitting Antuofermo with stiff jabs and uppercuts, finally knocking him down briefly in the third round. More skin opened up on his right eye, leaving a large gash. With blood spouting, the fight was over after the end of the fourth round. It was over. After years of brawling and mauling, of bleeding, how much more could Antuofermo take? He retired from fighting after 54 fights, but he returned to the ring in 1984 with four wins and one loss in 1985.

He had fought through adversity, and he became the undisputed champion of the world. His will, toughness, resilience and courage were embedded in him since he was a young boy in Italy. His head was bloody but unbowed.

He was 'Invictus'.

CAREER TOTALS

43 wins (32 KOs), 8 losses (4 KOs) and 1 draw.

VITO ANTUOFERMO – A DAY IN THE LIFE

What time do you get up in the morning?

6:00 am.

Do you do your roadwork in the morning?

I would either drive to the park to run or I would run along the beach at Coney Island.

How far did you run?

I liked to run 4–5 miles.

Do you stretch your body?

I stretched a lot. Full body. I stretched my arms and neck and head.

What do you do after you run?

I stretched a lot after I run.

What do you eat for breakfast?

A:: I liked 3 fried eggs, sausage and bacon. Orange juice.

What do you do after eating?

I walked. I liked to walk after eating.

How many days do you go to the gym?

5 or 6 depending on my training. I didn't go to the gym on Sundays, I went for a run.

What is your favourite exercise you do in the gym?

Sparring. I loved to spar.

What time do you go to the gym?

I would go to Bobby Gleasons gym at 1:00 pm to around 3:00 pm. I would go back at 7:00 pm.

What time do you finish in the gym?

I finished in the evening around 9:00 pm.

What do you eat for dinner?

I liked to eat steak. I would have a 35-ounce steak, and I would eat around 2 pounds (900 grams) a day. I would eat salads and vegetables, and I had water and juices.

Do you have a hobby or what do you like to do for fun?

I trained all the time, so I didn't have much time for nothing. I ate. I slept, and I got ready to fight. I liked to go out on a Friday and Saturday to a disco to go dancing.

Did you ever have a job?

I worked hard all my life. I worked for Coca Cola, working under their trucks. I always worked when I was boxing. I worked unloading ships and I was a crane operator for the port authority.

What time do you go to sleep?

10:00 pm.

NON-SPARRING DAYS

- Stretching. Full body (arms, neck and head) 20 minutes.
- Heavy Bag – 6 x 3-minute hard rounds. 1 minute rest in between.
- Speed Bag – 3 rounds x 3 minutes.
- Jump rope – 3 rounds x 3 minutes.

Stomach exercises:

- Sit ups x 60 of.
- Sit ups while getting hit by a 20-pound medicine ball x 60.
- Jump rope – 3 rounds x 3 minutes with a 1-minute rest between rounds.

SPARRING DAYS

- Stretching – Full body (arms, neck and head) 20 minutes.
- Shadow Box – 2 rounds x 3 minutes with a 1-minute rest between rounds.
- Sparring – 4–6 rounds progressing to 7, 8 and 9 rounds. (3 sparring partners)
- Heavy bag – 3 rounds x 3 minutes with a 1-minute rest between rounds.
- Jump rope – 3 rounds x 3 minutes with a 1-minute rest between rounds.
- Stomach exercises:
- Sit ups x 60*

* Sit ups while being hit by a 20-pound medicine ball

- Jump rope – 6 minutes.

GERR

GERRY COONEY

'A Gentleman in New York'

BIOGRAPHY

As I walked along the snow-covered sidewalk the streets were eerily quiet, with only the desperate and unfortunates out tonight. As I walked around the corner I braced myself as the snow was falling and the Arctic wind ripped through my clothes and into my bones. I looked up at the sign above me as I shook myself like a dog and I stepped inside the old dive bar that was 'Jimmy's Corner'.

I ordered a coke and spoke to the old guy behind the bar. We talked about the fights and the fighters whose photos were covering the walls, and I told him I was here to meet a fighter called Gerry Cooney. The man raised his eyebrows and smiled, saying "Now that guy could punch".

Just as the man hunched over to wash some glasses, the door opened and in walked Cooney. The snow had stuck to his hair and the thick collar of his coat as he smiled, shaking himself off. I walked towards him and shook his warm hand. I was happy and relieved that he was here, and I thanked him for meeting me. As I looked out the window the snow was heavy and it was falling almost horizontal and I wondered how the hell would I get back to my hotel, but I couldn't think of anywhere else I would rather be. We talked, and he talked, and I listened to his stories and as I listened, Cooney's eyes smiled as he spoke.

That was a long time ago, but I'll always remember the snow that night and the icebergs floating down the Hudson River but mostly I'll remember the warmth of the gentleman I met in New York, Gerry Cooney.

Gerry Cooney was born in 1956 and grew up in a working class, Irish Catholic household in Long Island, New York.

Growing up, Cooney and his brother Tom, were forced to fight each other in the backyard by their father as he watched them go at it, testing their fighting Irish spirit, while teaching them how to throw a hook, as they bloodied each other's nose. To finish, he would get them to hammer out drills on the heavy bag in the basement until he saw enough for one day.

Cooney and his brother would go into the amateurs, with the 6'6, fifteen-year-old training at the YMCA, eventually campaigning in fifty-seven contests with only two losses. Both brothers competed and won in two New York Golden Gloves championship, but their father pushed each of them for more which lead to frustration, bitterness, and anger.

Cooney left home and not long after, he was told that his father was sick and after watching him deteriorate and die, he decided to stop training and find a job.

He followed in his father's footsteps, finding a job as a steel worker in construction for a while but Cooney decided to go back to the gym and box again. It was in him.

He made the trip down to Manhattan to the old Bobby Gleason's Gym where he met the trainer, Victor Valle, and the two worked together and eventually they would become inseparable, with the ex-fighter igniting a spark which became a flame, deep inside Cooney's belly, just when he needed it. Echoes of his father's voice floated away like a phantom in the night as a new chapter began. Not long after their first meeting, he turned professional in 1977.

Cooney fought anyone they put in front of him, fighting seven times a year, with most of his fights never going past the fourth round.

In the gym, Valle was always there, always in the moment, giving instructions to the tough Irish slugger from Huntington, Long Island.

It was now 1980, and Cooney was on a 22-fight winning streak. Next up was the veteran tough guy, Jimmy Young. Young had been in tough hard fights with Michael Dokes, Ossie Ocasio, Ken Norton, George Foreman, Ron Lyle, Muhammad Ali, and Earnie Shavers, winning and losing on points with his only knockout loss to Shavers in 1973.

In the fight, Cooney battered the cagey and experienced Young to the body, hitting him cleanly with big left hooks and uppercuts, leaving him bleeding from his right eye, and struggling to see, forcing the stoppage after the fourth round. Five months later, he took out the 6'3 durable Ron Lyle in devastating fashion, overwhelming him with a fast start, accurate uppercuts, and knocking him out with a left rip to the body in the first round. All the talk was Cooney fighting the WBC champion, Larry Holmes, but it was announced that Ken Norton was next. The fight was to be staged at Madison Square Garden in the May of 1981, and Norton was seen by many as a dangerous fight for Cooney. The fighting Marine had won the WBC heavyweight title, and he had shared the ring with Muhammad Ali three times, shattering his jaw and beating him in 1973 to then go the distance with Ali in tough hard fights. He faced the might of George Foreman, being destroyed in two rounds in 1974. He then went fifteen gruelling rounds with Jimmy Young, and Larry Holmes in tough close fights. In 1979, he was knocked out by a thunderous punch from Earnie Shavers in the first round, but he kept fighting on, beating Randall 'Tex' Cobb on points in his last fight in November 1980.

While waiting for the introductions, the 6'3 Norton in his fiftieth fight, looked as strong as ever, defined and lean, with his body glistening in the lights, while Cooney in the corner, bouncing from toe to toe, his wide shoulders and long legs, looking more like a basketball player than a boxer.

As the bell rang, Cooney moved forward pushing the jab out then bang, Cooney caught Norton with a straight right hand that sent him reeling backwards to the ropes. Norton tried to duck under the oncoming punches, but he was caught flush by a blistering barrage of crisp thudding punches to his head and while the ropes, doing him no favours, held his 225-pound (102- kilo) body up, his knees buckled beneath him, with Cooney finishing him off in a brutal fifty-four seconds of the first round.

Ken Norton never fought again.

After going through years of fighting in the shadows as Muhammad Ali's sparring partner, the man known as 'The Easton Assassin' wanted some bread but received only stone. In 1978, Larry Holmes beat Ken Norton for the WBC heavyweight title, and he continued on with an impressive thirty-nine unbeaten run, (with twenty-nine KOs) beating Earnie Shavers, Alfredo Evangelista, Mike Weaver, Muhammad Ali, Trevor Berbick, and Leon Spinks along the way. Gerry Cooney would be his fortieth fight and his twelfth defence of his title. For Cooney, this fight would be thirteen months of inactivity, and thirteen months of broken promises, of phone calls and conversations of ifs, buts and maybes.

The Holmes fight was held in the 100-degree Fahrenheit (38 Celsius) heat of Las Vegas in the outdoor arena at Caesars Palace. In the fight, Holmes boxed behind his signature and tremendously accurate jab, controlling the pace of the fight following up with his solid right hand while Cooney threw his trademark left hook to the body and head of the champion. Cooney was sent to the canvas in the second round, but he recovered quickly. Holmes knew Cooney had been inactive, but he also knew he had never been beyond eight rounds in a fight, so he stuck and moved, patiently waiting for Cooney to tire and leave his guard down in the later rounds. Cooney was tiring and he was penalised for going low and as exhaustion started to affect the legs, Holmes agility, speed and power proved to be too much, hurting Cooney with a barrage of punches that opened a cut on his left eye, finally stopping him in the thirteenth round.

Cooney left boxing and lived his life. He returned two years later, winning two fights to then disappear again. Cooney came back in 1986 with another knockout win to then go into training camp to get ready for the unbeaten, 30-win champion, Michael Spinks.

While Cooney was away from the limelight of heavyweight boxing, the undisputed light heavyweight champion of the world, Michael Spinks had moved up in weight and beat the 48-win, unbeaten Larry Holmes by a sensational unanimous decision to then beat him again in 1986.

Spinks v Cooney was set for June 1987 in Atlantic City.

In the fight, the much bigger Cooney was relying on doubling up with his jab, and throwing his wide left hook while Spinks was throwing awkward punches in bunches, counterpunching Cooney as the fight went on. Cooney kept coming forward, but he was getting hit as Spinks pot shotted and hustled his way inside with a stinging two fisted relentless attack that took its toll on the 230-pound (104-kilo) Cooney. In the fifth round, Spinks began to connect with accurate left and right hands, which stunned and hurt Cooney, putting him down twice. Cooney got up quickly and stood flat footed as Spinks moved in with heavy fire, ending with hard uppercuts until the referee stepped in at 2:51 of the round to save the brave Cooney from further punishment.

Gerry Cooney again left the sport of boxing while Michael Spinks fought on until 1988, facing the ferocious Mike Tyson in Atlantic City, where Spinks was taken apart in ninety-one seconds of the first round.

He would never fight again.

Cooney came back to fight the forty-one-year-old George Foreman in January 1990, but he was clubbed and walked down by the plodding, 253-pound (114-kilo) powerhouse, with Foreman knocking him down from a big right hand and then six more unanswered clubbing punches. Cooney rose to his feet and Foreman casually stepped in and loaded up with a huge thunderbolt left uppercut that took everything out of him as he collapsed on the canvas in the second round. It was a devastating punch, and it would be the last punch Cooney would ever take.

What time do you get up in the morning?
5:30 am (My Dad woke me up to run.)

Do you do your roadwork in the morning?
Around six.

Do you stretch your body?
A little bit.

How far do you run?
3–5 miles depending on how far away the fight was.

What did you do after your run?
I would do some stomach work. I would go on my bicycle then have a rest.

What did you eat for breakfast?
Eggs, bacon, potatoes and orange juice. Water.

What do you do after eating?
In the early days, I would go to school. Later, I rested until I went to the gym.

How many days do you train in the gym?
5 days boxing. Sometimes 6 depending on training and what we were doing. Sunday, we went to church.

What is your favourite exercise in the gym?
I liked to box. Spar. I started in a gym in Long Island then when I went pro, I moved.

What time do you go to the gym?
I would go to the gym at 3:00 pm. I would stay there all day.

What time do you finish in the gym?
I trained for 2 hours but I hung out there until around 9:00 pm.

What do you eat for dinner?
I liked chicken, steak, pasta. I'm Irish so we ate a lot of potatoes, and I drank water. I would go for a walk after eating.

Do you have a hobby or what do you do for fun?
It was all boxing. I would go for walks. Talk to people. I liked being outside and I liked being in the ocean. I liked out on a boat.

Did you ever have a job?
I worked in construction before I turned professional.

What time do you go to sleep?
11:00 pm.

NON-SPARRING DAYS

- Shadow Box. 2–3 rounds x 3 minutes.
- (1 minute break in between all rounds.)
- Heavy bag 4–6–8 rounds x 3 minutes.
- Jump rope 2–3 rounds x 3 minutes.
- Speed bag. 2 rounds x 3 minutes.
- Focus pads 4 rounds x 3 minutes.
- Jump rope. 3 rounds x 3 minutes.
- Shadow Box in the ring 3 rounds x 3 minutes.

(I did my stomach work after running).

- Go for a shower. Massage if I was tight.

SPARRING DAYS

NOTE: All exercises have 1-minute breaks between rounds

- Jump rope. 2–3 rounds x 3 minutes.
- Speed bag. 2–3 rounds x 3 minutes.
- Pad work 3 rounds x 3 minutes.
- Sparring. 6–8 hard rounds x 3 minutes.
- Heavy Bag. 2–3 rounds x 3 minutes.
- Double End Bag – 2 rounds x 3 minutes.
- Shadow Box. 3 rounds x 3 minutes.
- Speed Bag 2 rounds x 3 minutes.

(I would get a massage when I felt tight legs shoulders and back.)

(I would do exercises to build the tendons in my shoulders)

(I would go swimming)

YAQUI LOPEZ

'Blood and Dirt'

BIOGRAPHY

The twelve-year-old boy jumped from his bed as the rays of light crept through the cracks of the room. There had been tough hard days but today was going to be a good day for the boy. As he walked barefooted out on to the dustbowl land, the sun made him squint through narrowed eyes until he walked into the passage of shade that lead to the Bull Ring.

Living under the ring, he had heard the roar of the crowd, he could feel the power of the bull moving through the ground, and he could smell death in the air. The boy had dreamt of this many times and today in a few hours, he would face the beast. As he stood still, he reached down and picked up a handful of dirt and rubbed it into his hands as he imagined what could be.

Blood and dirt.

The savage, thousand-pound bull snorted steam from its nostrils as it circled and stomped the ground, waiting, staring and trying to resist what it had been bred for. Rage, chaos and death. The boy stood there bravely in defiance as the bull charged him, head down, jerking violently, twisting itself around, hooking it's horn into the boy's right ankle, lifting him into the air where he crashed into the dirt.

All there was, was blood and dirt. In seconds his foot was shattered, and his dream was crushed.

Alvaro Yaqui Lopez was born in 1951 in the Mexican mining town of Zacatecas. His Mother and Father made the move across the border and worked hard to settle in the small rural town of Linden in California. They scraped up some money which paid for their boy Yaqui to join them when he was fourteen years old. He went to school for six months but he quickly realised that it wasn't for him, so he found a job, working the fields alongside hundreds of immigrants, picking peaches and cherries and carrying buckets of fruit all day, with little water and no shade in the hot Californian sun, for a pittance of seventy-five cents an hour. It was a means to an end and a long hard road to somewhere.

Lopez found boxing in the most unlikely way after moving to Stockton, which was one of chance, love and fate. Sometimes in life, the stars align and for the young Mexican, Cupid's arrow struck as he found the girl that would become his love for the next fifty years. This chance at love would also bring together another partnership. This one between Beatrice's father and Lopez – an entirely different partnership of blood, sweat, struggle and violence, and a loyalty that would prevail for fourteen years, in and out of the boxing ring.

Jack Cruz knew a bit about the business of fighting. He was a boxing promoter who had the reputation of matching his fighters in tough fights. Lopez asked him if he could show him how to box and move around and two weeks later, the nineteen-year-old had his first amateur fight.

After fifteen contests, Lopez turned professional in 1972.

Cruz wasted no time, matching Lopez with strong fighters in eight to ten round fights where he was either going to be the bull or the Matador. Tough fights with Al Bolden seeing the two fighters down three times each to lose on points to then go on an eighteen-fight winning streak including beating Bolden in their rematch.

A good win against Hildo Silva proved Lopez could go twelve hard rounds, to then lose in a setback fight to Jesse Burnett in his twenty ninth contest in 1975.

Lopez came back two months later and beat Burnett to fight his way into contention for a world title shot for the Englishman, John Conteh's WBC light heavyweight belt. Conteh, was the son of a west African father and an Irish mother, and he was born and bred in Liverpool. He was a tremendously skilled boxer who had won a gold medal as a middleweight at the 1970 commonwealth Games in Edinburgh, Scotland to then turn professional in 1971 and win the European, British and Commonwealth light heavyweight titles in 1973. These hard-fought wins put him in line to face the tough Argentinian slugger, Jorge Ahumada for the vacant WBC light heavyweight title in London. After another hard, gruelling fight, Conteh used his superior boxing skills by throwing hard jabs to try and control the Argentinian's lunges, in a war of attrition, with the English fighter connecting with big uppercuts to win on points over a fast-paced fifteen round contest to become a world champion at the age of twenty three, and only the third British man to win the light heavyweight title, joining Bob Fitzsimmons and Freddie Mills in the history books.

Going into the fight, the champion had injured his right hand, breaking it twice in fights, which left him needing surgery and a bone graft. Inactivity, ring rust and a hungry brawling Mexican in Lopez definitely wasn't what the doctor ordered for the second defence of his beloved title.

The fight was held in Copenhagen, Denmark in the October of 1976. In the fight, Lopez fought hard, pushing forward with Conteh using his jab and boxing to great effect, but also being gun shy with his right hand. After fifteen rounds, it was a close fight with the difference being the accuracy of Conteh's left jab, followed by his left hook, which was evident in the final round, which was enough to retain his title.

Conteh would go on to win but be stripped of his world title to then challenge the durable Croatian, Mate Parlov in Belgrade, losing by a controversial split decision in 1978. The Englishman would challenge the teak tough warrior, Matthew Saad Muhammad for his WBC light heavyweight title in Atlantic City, losing over fifteen gruelling rounds to then be knocked out in the rematch in his final year in the sport in 1980.

Lopez fought on. He knew inside that he belonged, and the fire burned inside him. He fought nine times in 1977, and travelling to Italy to challenge the WBA light heavyweight champion from Argentina, Victor Galindez.

In the fight, Lopez fought a tremendous fight, pressing forward and doubling up with the jab and going to the champions body to take his legs, but after going fifteen rounds, the judges gave the fight to Galindez, by scoring a ridiculous unanimous decision. Galindez fought a good fight in spurts through the middle rounds, but Lopez fought with an ongoing tenacity, landing more punches, while the champion seemed happy to coast through the championship distance. Yaqui Lopez deserved better than that as he graciously walked back to the dressing room, with a chorus of protests behind him echoing through the crowd, he should have had his hand raised as the light heavyweight champion of the world.

Lopez went back to Stockton beating whoever they put in front of him, including an impressive display against the favoured contender, Mike Rossman in New York, battering him to the body and head, forcing a corner stoppage after the sixth round. This win earned him the right to go back to Italy and face Galindez in the rematch. After another fifteen rounds, the champion retained his title and once again, Lopez returned home with his head held high, wondering what tomorrow would bring.

After beating Jesse Burnett Lopez was matched to face the hard as nails, Philadelphia fighter, Matthew Franklin for the light heavyweight NABF title.

In the fight, Lopez was hurt, and then came back to hurt Franklin repeatedly, going to the body and head, with a two-fisted onslaught that had him on the ropes, covering up and waiting for his turn. Lopez threw everything he could, but Franklin fought back with unbelievable grit, courage and will, to hurt Lopez. With Lopez's right eye completely closed and blinded, Franklin opened up with accurate punch combinations that had the courageous Lopez fighting off the ropes, throwing punches and willing himself to win.

In the end, the referee had seen enough, and he stopped the fight at the end of the eleventh round. Franklin won, but both fighters had given a piece of themselves in the ring that night and each would give much more in time.

Franklin became world champion then changed his name to Matthew Saad Muhammad in 1979 to go on to beating John Conteh on points to then knock the proud 'Scouser 'out in the rematch in 1980.

Lopez had five fights in 1979, losing to James Scott by a ten round points decision in a fight that was staged inside a prison to end the year. He came back again, winning and hoping for another chance. Muhammad was now the WBC champion, and he promised Lopez that when he became the champion of the world, he would give the tough Mexican warrior a rematch.

He would be true to his word.

The fight was held in the summer of 1980 in New Jersey. This was the fourth defence of Muhammad's world title, and this also marked the fourth attempt at a world title for Lopez.

In the fight, Lopez was telling anyone who would listen that he was going to box and move but as soon as the champion opened up, Lopez's plan evaporated, as he engaged in a gruelling relentless war of attrition, of courage, and pride. Lopez was boxing brilliantly, doubling up with his jab, throwing left hook rips to Muhammad's body, forcing him backwards. The WBC champion was throwing the more powerful punches that stunned Lopez, but the Mexican proved he was in the best condition of his career by taking heavy fire in furious exchanges and coming back with his own shots that hurt Muhammad. Lopez had thrown everything at the Philadelphia strongman, and by the twelfth round, he was exhausted. Arm weary and his legs starting to go, Lopez never stopped fighting, but he was being countered and taking punishment, Muhammad landed with a big right hand in the thirteenth round which was the beginning of the end. Muhammad came out strong in the fourteen, battering Lopez and knocking him down three times to then land a hard right hand that put him down and out in the fourteenth round of a brutal fight. The two fights between these two warriors will be remembered for their brilliant brutality, their bravery and a testament to the power of the human spirit.

Matthew Saad Muhammad fought on, but he would never again be the same fighter, fighting on way too long. He had gone to the well too many times, retiring after eighteen years in 1992. He passed away in May 2014. He was fifty-nine years old.

Yaqui Lopez could have walked away from boxing but instead, he faced the unbeaten 1976 Olympic Gold medallist, Michael Spinks, losing by knockout in the seventh round.

Lopez fought another sixteen fights, facing future Cruiser weight champion ST Gordon, and Australian, Tony Mundine eventually moving up to fight at cruiserweight where he challenged the WBC champion, Carlos De Leon. Lopez received a bad cut to his right eye, forcing the fight to be stopped in the fourth round, giving the fight to Mundine.

Lopez returned a few months later, losing to Bash Ali in 1984. After seventy-six fights, Lopez walked away. He had fought with heart, passion and a never-ending determination that came from deep inside him.

There were so many hard fights.

Lopez bled for glory, in the toughest sport of blood and dirt.

CAREER TOTALS

Lopez retired with a fight record of 61 wins (39 KOs), 15 losses (6 KOs) and no draws.

"I TRAINED HARD EVERY DAY AND I FOUGHT WITH HEART. I HOPE I AM REMEMBERED FOR THE FIGHTS I HAD. I AM HAPPY."

YAQUI LOPEZ

YAQUI LOPEZ – A DAY IN THE LIFE

What time do you get up in the morning?

3:30 am.

Do you do your roadwork in the morning?

3:30am – 5:00 am.

Do you stretch your body?

Yes. Full body stretch.

How far do you run?

I ran 7 miles a day.

What do you do after your run?

I would shower, eat then go to work at 6:00 am.

What do you eat for breakfast?

I had raw eggs every morning. Squeezed lemon. Orange juice.

How many days do you train in the gym?

5 days in the gym. Saturdays and Sundays, I ran 9 miles.

What is your favourite exercise in the gym?

I loved to jump rope and hit the speed bag.

What time do you go to the gym?

I arrived at the gym at 4:00 pm. My trainer waited for me to get ready to spar but sometimes for sparring, we would drive to Oakland and San Francisco. We used 5 sparring partners going 15 rounds.

What time do you finish in the gym?

6:00 pm, working out.

What do you eat for dinner?

Salads, fish chicken. No red meat. Orange juice, hot tea with lemon.

Do you have a hobby or what do you do for fun?

I played racquetball, basketball, and baseball and I liked watching sports.

Did you ever have a job?

Yes. I drove a forklift in a cannery in Stockton. I loaded pallets of cherry tomatoes. I worked from 6:00 am until 2:00 pm every day.

What time do you go to sleep?

9:00 pm.

- Stretching full body 15 minutes.
- Jump rope 4 rounds 12 minutes non-stop.
- Heavy bag. 4 rounds x 3 minutes (1 minute Break in between each round) Trainer would hold the bag as I dug in left and right rips. (body shots)
- Speed bag. 3 rounds. 9 minutes non-stop.
- Push ups 50 . Go all the way to the floor and up again.
- Sit ups. 50 Using the medicine ball.
- Neck strengthening. Hands behind my back with my head taking my weight on the gym mat. Moved my head forwards and backwards until tired.
- Put a head harness on and attach a seven-pound weight which was hanging down from harness strap. Moved my head up and down and side to side.

Note: Lopez would begin sparring 25 days out from the fight. Hard sparring of 15 rounds x 3 minutes throughout with no sparring 5 days before the fight – keeping loose and to make the weight easy.

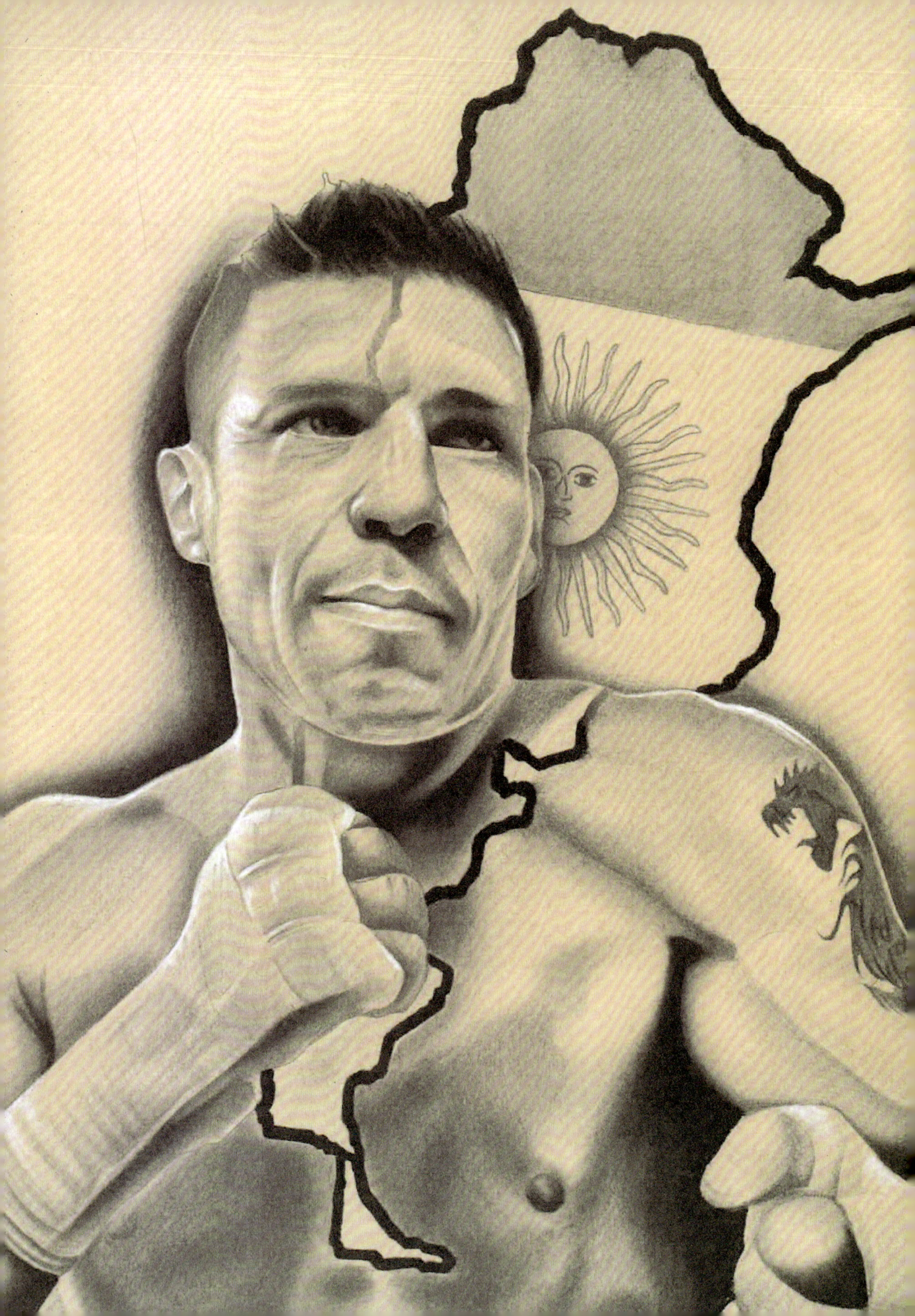

SERGIO MARTINEZ

'Campeon'

BIOGRAPHY

Sergio Martinez was born in the industrial port city of Avellaneda near Buenos Aires, Argentina in 1975. As a child, growing up in an area that was deprived of the most basic everyday things to survive, Martinez would play soccer in the overpopulated barrio of 'La Villa' before moving to Quilmes.

In 1994, after asking his uncle to teach him how to box, Martinez began campaigning soon after as an amateur, competing in 41 contests with one loss and one draw over a two-year period. There was talk of the twenty-two-year-old boxing his way to represent his beloved Argentina in the Sydney Olympics in 2000, but in the end, he decided to turn professional as time waited for no one.

Martinez made his debut as a paid fighter in December 1997, going undefeated in seventeen fights to then travel to Las Vegas in 2000, to face the twenty-one-year-old Mexican puncher, Antonio Margarito.

Known for his aggressive attacking style, fighting grown men in the beer and piss stained, cock fighting bars in Tijuana, Margarito was a dangerous welterweight who was being primed as the next Mexican star.

In the fight, Margarito proved to be too experienced, too strong, and too much, making Martinez miss and leaving himself wide open to the relentless body punches and two-fisted, headhunting attack from the Mexican tornado, taking the inexperienced Argentinian boxer out with only seconds to go in the seventh round.

Martinez returned home to Argentina and fought on, learning and working hard to keep his dream alive.

In time, he would prove to himself that he could be a champion, beating anyone that was put in front of him. After moving to Spain, he was matched to fight the Englishman, Richard Williams in Manchester in 2003 for his IBO super welterweight title, taking the fight on eight days notice.

Going into the fight, Martinez had been unbeaten in twelve fights. Williams had been busy in recent years leading up to the fight, winning the Commonwealth junior middleweight title, to then go on to stop the Australian brawler, Shannon Taylor, winning the IBO junior middleweight belt. He added the WBF junior middleweight title to his collection, stopping the durable Russian, Andrey Pestryayev in his last outing in 2003.

Martinez was going into the lion's den as a big underdog, an unknown fighter, with many seeing him as mere cannon fodder.

In the fight, the champion came out trying for the big knockout punch, but Martinez boxed well behind his solid southpaw jab, catching Williams with slashing accurate hooks which had him going backwards to the ropes. Williams came out firing in the third round with a two-fisted attack, landing a hard left cross to then nail Martinez with his famed right hand, knocking the Argentinian down. Martinez jumped up quickly and recovered well to out box the champion. From there, Martinez's timing, distance and ring generalship was evident, piling on the pressure in the championship rounds and leaving the Englishman exhausted and down in the final round to win by a unanimous decision.

Next up for the new champion was Adrian Stone. Known as 'The Predator', the 5'7 man from Bristol could bang, with twenty-six knockouts in his thirty-three-fight career. He was as exciting as he was experienced, having faced the talented welterweights Vernon Forest in 1998, and Shane Mosley in 2001.

In the fight, Martinez was too slick and pinpoint accurate with his jab, showing tremendous footwork and boxing skills that eventually took their toll. Stone showed great courage, but he was busted up, broken and knocked out in the twelfth round. Stone would never fight again.

It was now 2004. A rematch was signed for Richard Williams to try and get his old title back. The fight was held in Belfast at the historic Kings Hall and in the fight, Martinez proved to be too much, breaking down Williams with his jab, and hard left hands in a dominant performance that forced a corner stoppage at the end of the ninth round.

Sergio 'Maravilla' Martinez continued on to a twenty-eight-fight, unbeaten journey which lasted an incredible nine years.

It was now 2009. Martinez went to Florida to face the big punching Puerto Rican, Kermit Cintron, defending his WBC junior middleweight interim title. The twenty-nine-year-old Cintron was known as 'The Killer' and he was a former world champion with an impressive record of 30 fights with 27 knockouts and only two losses.

In a bizarre and controversial fight, Martinez once again used his legs and his superior footwork along with his ramrod jab to out box Cintron. Martinez won most of the rounds in a convincing display of skill, speed and power, knocking Cintron down with a huge left-hand punch at the end of the seventh round. The referee counted Cintron to the count of nine and arguably a slower count to reach ten as Cintron rose to his feet. The referee waved off the fight as the round ended. After Cintron and his team protested, saying the knockdown was from a head clash, unbelievably the fight resumed for the eighth round. Martinez fought the remaining rounds, with his hands down, taunting Cintron while out boxing, out classing and out punching the Puerto Rican. Martinez was deducted a point in the final round, despite dominating the twelfth round and the entire twelve-round contest.

The officiating judges saw things much different, with one judge giving Martinez the win with a 116–110 score and the other two judges scoring the fight a *scandalous* 113–113, a draw.

After a few months off, Martinez returned to the gym and trained harder than ever. The bitterness of that night had been and gone and now the Argentinian champion had to prepare for the serious challenge of the six-foot-two Paul Williams.

Williams was known as 'The Punisher', beating Antonio Margarito, Sharmba Mitchell, and Winky Wright, with his only loss to the Puerto Rican Southpaw, Carlos Quintana on points in 2008. He was a big, strong southpaw with fast hands, who consistently threw accurate, high volume, quality punches to his opponent's head and body, systematically breaking them down and knocking them out.

In the fight, Williams came out throwing punches with conviction with the strategy that pressure and boxing from the outside would be the key to victory in the fight. Martinez had to get inside and throw left hooks to the head and go to the body to take Williams legs. The first round was exciting as it was dramatic, with Williams catching Martinez with a punch that caught him on the side of the ear, stunning him as he went down to the canvas. Martinez jumped up quickly and recovered quickly to fire back with a big left hook to then hammer Williams with a punch perfect right hook that sent him down, sprawling into the ropes to finish the round. From there on in, it was a back-and-forth battle, with both champions taking big shots to each come back in defiance. Martinez was outstanding as he worked inside, counterpunching Williams with hard left and right hooks, to then be stunned by 'The Punisher'.

Going into the seventh round, the fight was even and with Williams bleeding and Martinez breathing hard, both fighters gave no quarter in a fight for the ages. Martinez won the eighth, hurting Williams to the head and body. Round nine was close. Ten was Martinez's round due to landing a huge left hand that had Williams in trouble. Round eleven was brutal with both men trading body punches in the centre of the ring, leaving Martinez exhausted but unbelievably, he continued to throw hard left hooks to win the round. In a war of attrition, the will to win was the difference in the fight. Both fighters gave everything. Martinez finished stronger and his will was undeniable. With the ringside judges scores of 114–114, 115–113, and a disgraceful 119–110, Paul Williams was declared the winner.

It was the fight of the year and the crime of the century.

Martinez returned in early 2010, to face the big punching WBC middleweight champion of the world, Kelly Pavlik. The man known as 'The Ghost' had been accustomed to relieving people of their senses since 2000, with only one loss in thirty-seven fights to Bernard Hopkins in 2008.

In the fight, Pavlik came in as the much bigger man, with the aim of bullying the Argentinian to the ropes and unleashing his famed two-fisted weapons on the smaller man. Martinez came into the ring at an agile one hundred and sixty pounds, with the hope that his movement, speed and skill would be the difference.

As Pavlik stalked, throwing the jab while looking for the opening to land his signature powerful punch, Martinez moved and pot shotted the champion with accurate combinations, winning the early rounds. Pavlik imposed his size in the middle rounds, catching Martinez off balance, as he connected with a short right hand punch that sent the challenger down in the seventh round. Martinez was unfazed and came back strongly with a dazzling display, leaving Pavlik cut over both eyes.

In the end, Martinez was too good, too fast and too accurate, beating Pavlik by a unanimous decision to become the WBC and WBO middleweight champion of the world. Pavlik retired in 2012.

As champion, Martinez could have fought a long list of fighters, but he wanted Paul Williams, and the fight was signed for the November of 2010 in Atlantic City.

Williams had, on paper, defeated Kermit Cintron in a contest at 154 pounds (69.8 kilos) that ended abruptly in the fourth round after the Puerto Rican stumbled awkwardly after engaging with Williams to then tumble through the ropes, injuring himself and leaving the arena on a stretcher.

Williams trained hard, coming in as the bigger man at middleweight, and saying he would be more dominant this time. Martinez was quiet.

In the fight, the sold-out crowd expected another display of beautiful brutality from both men. Martinez gave them just that, knocking out Williams cold with a left-hand thunderbolt punch he didn't see coming in the second round. Martinez, in his fiftieth fight, was the number one middleweight in the world.

'Maravilla' would fight on, defending his titles, knocking out tough challengers in Serhiy Dzinziruk, Darren Barker, and Matthew Macklin, to then face the huge middleweight, Julio Cesar Chavez in September 2012. Chavez went into the fight, undefeated in forty-seven contests.

In the fight, Chavez inspired by the thousands of Mexican fans and his famous father at ringside watching, fought hard, opening up on the inside and going to the champions body to take his legs and movement away. Martinez never took a backward step, counter punching and landing hard jabs and left hooks to the much bigger man from Culiacan, Mexico. Chavez and Martinez went to war in the final round, with the champion being hurt badly by a big left hook, which had him staggering and going down. The proud champion rose to his feet and Chavez poured on the pressure with a late onslaught, but Martinez fought his way through it, opting to stand and slug it out until the final bell rang. Martinez won the fight with skill and the will to win, but most of all he fought with the heart of a champion.

Martinez went back to Argentina to fight in front of his people. He could have arranged an easy fight for his long-overdue home coming but, true to form, he took on the challenge from the hard man from England, Martin Murray.

The fight was staged at a soccer stadium in Buenos Aires with a sellout crowd of 52,000 people in attendance to see their countryman put on a show. Going into the fight, Martinez had been unable to train properly while waiting for his left hand to heal after it was broken in the Chavez fight. The unbeaten Murray had nothing to lose and everything to gain and in the fight. The Englishman did whatever he could do to mitigate the fast hands and awkward movement of the thirty-eight-year-old champion. Martinez jabbed and moved with his hands down low, and Murray caught the champion with a solid left hook to then follow up with a straight right hand that sent the Argentinian down. Martinez recovered quickly and Murray couldn't capitalise on the moment or come close to realising his own dream of becoming a world champion. Martinez won the fight on points but after a long career in tough fights, his body was starting to break down.

After being away from boxing for over a year, Martinez came back to defend his WBC middleweight title against Miguel Cotto in New York in the June of 2014.

Martinez entered the ring wearing knee braces on both legs while the Puerto Rican bounced around on his toes.

Cotto came out, snapping his solid jab, knocking Martinez's head back. Martinez was then caught by a hard left hook that wobbled him, to then be clocked with a big left rip to the body. Martinez was staggered and knocked to the canvas three times in the round. Martinez tried desperately to hold on to yesterday, but his legs betrayed him. Cotto controlled the pace and the centre of the ring, all the while boxing and making Martinez use his legs, and he systematically broke down the courageous champion by the end of the ninth round. Martinez did not come out for the tenth round. It was over. Martinez retired from the sport and enjoyed life.

He returned in 2020, winning six contests, retiring for good in 2023.

Sergio Martinez fought with pride and passion, with dignity and grace. An underdog. A warrior, and a 'Campeon' in the ring and in life.

CAREER TOTALS

Martinez retired with a fight record of 57 wins (32 KOs) 3 losses (2 KOs) and 2 draws.

SERGIO MARTINEZ – A DAY IN THE LIFE

What time do you get up in the morning?

4:00 am.

Do you do your roadwork in the morning?

Yes. I run at 5:00 am.

Do you stretch your body?

Yes. I stretch my whole body.

How far do you run?

8 miles.

What do you do after you run?

I rest my body.

What do you eat for breakfast?

I like bacon, eggs, avocado, water and coffee.

What do you do after eating?

I go for a sleep before I get ready to train.

How many days do you go to the gym?

6 days. Sunday off.

What is your favourite exercise in the gym?

I loved the heavy bag.

What time do you go to the gym?

4:00 pm.

What time do you finish in the gym?

Around 7:00 pm. I would shower and get a massage.

What do you eat for dinner?

I like fish, beef and salads. Water, juices and coffee.

Do you have a hobby or what do you like to do for fun?

I love watching comedies. Argentinian comedy, movies and I like driving fancy cars. I also enjoyed riding my bike and when I was younger, I played football.

Did you ever have a job?

Yes of course. I worked in a night club. I worked in construction, and I washed dishes to get some money.

What time do you go to sleep?

I go to sleep at 3am. I only sleep for 1 or 2 hours every night.

NON-SPARRING DAYS

- Stretching – full body 20 minutes.
- Shadow box – 3 x 3-minute rounds with all exercises 1 minute break between each round.
- Heavy bag – 8–10 rounds x 3 minutes.
- Focus pad work – 3 rounds x 3 minutes.
- Sit ups / stomach work and weight and strength exercises on alternating days in camp.
- Massage and shower.

SPARRING DAYS

- Stretching – full body 20 minutes.
- Shadow box – 3 x 3 minutes (1 minute break in between each round)
- Heavy bag – 5 rounds x 3 minutes.
- Sparring – 6–8 rounds.

Note: sparring was once a week with 3 different sparring partners.

- Shadow box – 2 rounds x 3 minutes.
- Mondays, Wednesday, and Friday, 1200 of stomach exercises non-stop.
- Tuesday, Thursday and Saturday,
- 1500 of stomach exercises non-stop.
  Note: as training camp progressed, weight training/ strength exercises would be added into training on alternating days.
- Massage and shower.

DANNY LOPEZ

'Native Son'

BIOGRAPHY

Danny Lopez was born in an Indian reservation near the foot of the Uinta mountains in the Utah valley in 1952. Home to his people, the nomadic Ute, Uinta and Ouray tribes. He lived with his family in an area called Fort Duchesne which was a Fort originally built by the United States Army in 1886, as a measure to control the heightened tension in the area. The now abandoned and dilapidated walls have all but disappeared, but the memories of hardship and poverty still remain.

Lopez's father walked away leaving his mother to raise their eight young children, living in a small shack with little food and help from no one, it was a painfully hard life living within the reservation. Bitterly cold winters and hot humid summers, with sickness, famine and death all around as families lived below the poverty line.

Lopez' mother inevitably could no longer take the burden of caring for her children and the authorities intervened and split their family apart, placing them in multiple foster care homes.

As young children, Danny and his brothers were filled with a profound sadness, and they found it hard to trust people which later turned to anger inside, which lead to them getting into trouble. They would go to school where they began to wrestle, reaching the Utah state championships, before they took up boxing.

Danny's brother Ernie, was the first, showing great talent, then Danny followed him. They would train every day at 'Stan's Boxing Club' in Utah, while Danny watched and learned, competing in the amateurs.

After a while, Ernie decided to leave his teenage brothers and go and fight in California. Danny followed later in his brother's footsteps to Los Angeles, where they each chased their dream of being a champion. Danny's other brother's continued boxing in the amateurs, with Leonard going on to box in the military.

Lopez was now sixteen years old. He was training every day, and he had met a girl named Bonnie. Little did he know that his life would change, finding love, and a soulmate that would join him on a journey that would last the rest of his life.

After campaigning in forty amateur contests, Lopez turned professional in 1970, training and sparring at the Main Street Gym, at the age of eighteen, and making his debut in 1971.

Ernie 'Indian Red' Lopez went on to fight in sixty-one fights, facing Hedgemon Lewis three times, Chucho Garcia, Jose Napoles twice for his world title, Emile Griffith, Armando Muniz, and John H. Stracey in his final fight in 1974.

With 23 wins (with 22 knockouts) in his first three years, Danny Lopez was making a name for himself as an entertaining, exciting, raw talent who didn't know how to take a backward step, pressing forward and beating his opponents senseless with a volume of hard punches until they couldn't continue.

After beating the durable boxer Genzo Kurosawa in Los Angeles, in a fight that Lopez threw close to eighteen hundred punches, the man from Tokyo held on, losing by a wide decision over ten rounds, Lopez then took on the popular Mexican, Bobby Chacon in 1974. The fight was held in Los Angeles in front of 16,000 people. Lopez was outboxed, with Chacón's skill and speed of punch being the difference in the fight.

In the ninth round, Chacon came out firing right hand bombs that sent Lopez to the ropes, to then connect with twenty-one unanswered blows that sent Lopez down. With his legs gone, Lopez got to his feet quickly to then get hammered, leaving the referee to stop the fight.

He returned a few months later to beat Masanao Toyoshima to then be stopped by the wild swinging, underdog, Shig Fukuyama in a gruelling war at the Olympic Auditorium in Los Angeles. The Japanese brawler was cut and bleeding, fighting as a desperate man, throwing left hooks, and a two-fisted onslaught, hurting Lopez in the eighth round to end proceedings.

Lopez was then beaten on points by Octavio Gomez in early January 1975.

Lopez came back with a fire and determination inside, knocking out Chucho Castillo, Ruben Olivares, Sean O'Grady, Art Hafey and Octavio Gomez to win seven fights in a row. These impressive wins opened the door to a title shot against the Ghanaian WBC Featherweight champion of the world, David Kotey.

To win, he would need to go to Accra, Ghana, to face the champion and beat him convincingly to have any chance of victory.

In the fight, Kotey boxed and moved around the ring, pot shotting the American, hoping to take him into the trenches in the championship rounds. With jungle drums beating around the stadium, and 100,000 Ghanaians chanting and dancing in the heat and humidity of the overcrowded Accra Sports Stadium, Lopez was throwing the jab and the right hand loading up, trying to take the champion out as early as possible. Kotey stuck to his game plan, moving and keeping his two arms up in a tight defence, protecting his chin. Lopez was relentless, pushing Kotey backwards to the ropes, but he couldn't find the right hand to knock the supremely conditioned champion out.

In the end, after a long hard fight, Lopez was exhausted, but his arm was raised in victory. After thirty-five fights, Danny Lopez had realised his dream of becoming the WBC Featherweight champion of the world.

After a few fights defending his world title once against Jose Torres, Lopez fought Kotey in a rematch in Las Vegas in 1978. Going into the fight, Lopez's longtime manager, Howie Steindler was found dead, brutally murdered in his car.

In the fight, Lopez fought with patience, picking his punches, while chipping away at Kotey, cutting the ring off, while waiting for an opening and when it came, Lopez was too much for Kotey. A heavy assault of right hands put him down and out in the sixth round.

With no respite or time to celebrate, Lopez was matched with the durable Brazilian champion, Jose De Paulo.

In the fight, Lopez's pressure and two-fisted attack took effect, and as the rounds went on, the tough Guy from São Paulo began to fold. Lopez battered him with body punches and uppercuts, finishing with right- and left-hand thudding punches that took his heart, knocking him down in the sixth round. The brave challenger rose to his feet, but it was over when the towel was thrown into the ring.

He was then matched to fight the big punching Argentinian, Juan Domingo Malvarez in New Orleans. Malvarez had been fighting nine times a year and he was known for having a powerful left hand and he could box.

In the fight, Lopez was taking big punches in the first round from the man from Argentina, going down from a hard left right left combination. Once again, Lopez rose to his feet, but it was Malvarez who finished the round strong with solid combination punches. Lopez was stunned again early in the second round, but he never stopped coming forward, looking to land one of his own. Malvarez was boxing tremendously well until a thunderbolt right hand sent him crashing to the canvas. Lopez was on the brink of defeat again, but he came back, and knocked the hard punching Argentinian out cold, continuing with his mantra of, you hit me hard, I'll come back and hit you harder.

After a well-deserved break, Lopez faced the 29-fight, unbeaten Spanish pocket rocket, Roberto Castanon in Salt Lake City, knocking him out in two rounds.

It was then announced Lopez would be defending his title against the number one contender, Mike Ayala. The fight was held in Ayala's hometown of San Antonio, Texas.

Ayala had only lost one fight in twenty-three contests, and he was a good boxer, a pressure fighter and he was an exciting counterpuncher.

In the fight, Lopez targeted Ayala's body forcing him back to the ropes to then open up with strong thudding punches. Ayala seemed happy to be there to then fight his way off the ropes to hit Lopez with fast combinations to the body and head. It was a fire fight with neither fighter giving an inch. Lopez pawed Ayala with seven jabs then knocked him down in the seventh round with a straight right hand but the 5'4 Ayala recovered to finish the round throwing punches.

Ayala came out in the eighth round throwing hard punches which stunned the champion, but he kept coming forward. Ayala continued to fight off the ropes, landing big left hooks. It was a war. A close battle in close quarters. In the eleventh round, Ayala went down again, and the referee counted him out but unbelievably the timekeeper at ringside corrected the referee and telling him his count wasn't correct. The battle continued into round twelve with both warriors showing tremendous courage and heart. Lopez piled on the pressure, while taking fire but in the final round, he hit Ayala with two huge right hands which sent him down and out in the fifteenth round. It was a fight filled with drama, pride, passion, and guts. It was the fight of the year and a throwback fight for the ages.

When the war was over, Lopez went on a fishing and camping vacation to rest and recover. There was talk of Lopez going up in weight to challenge the Scottish world champion, Jim Watt, for his Lightweight title but in the end, Lopez, true to form, agreed to fight another tough fight, facing the puncher from the Dominican Republic, Jose Caba, just three months after the Ayala classic battle.

In the fight, Caba was connecting with head snapping punches in the first round and going into the second round, he was throwing solid jabs and wild hooks, but Lopez kept coming forward. With neither man willing to concede, Lopez stepped up his attack, suddenly catching Caba on the ropes, battering him until his legs dipped and his body was unable to react or stop himself from falling through the ropes. He recovered and jumped up to then be sent through the same ropes for a second time. Lopez finished him off in the third round.

Caba fought on, going the distance but losing to Eusebio Pedrosa in 1983. He then succumbed to a seventh-round stoppage by Barry McGuigan in Belfast 84.

Lopez could have fought anyone, but the fearless champion fought the twenty-one-year-old, Mexican, Salvador Sanchez in Phoenix, Arizona in February 1980.

In the fight, Lopez used his piston like jab to try and set up the big right hand. Sanchez moved superbly, counter punching and throwing left and right combinations as he controlled the tempo and staying off the ropes. Sanchez's boxing skills, and footwork were outstanding, as he moved around the ring, picking his punches. Lopez never stopped marching forward, but he was being picked off as his left eye was starting to close. With his eye cut and swelling, Sanchez took his time, punching through Lopez and eventually he broke down the courageous champion, hitting him with punches he couldn't see, to finally hit him with a big right hand and a heavy barrage of punches to end the fight in the thirteenth round. Salvador Sanchez was the WBC Featherweight champion of the world at the age of twenty-one.

Lopez was battered, bruised and cut over both eyes in the fight but the rematch was set for just a few months later in Las Vegas.

As Lopez healed, Sanchez beat Ruben Castillo in his first defence in April 1980.

It was too soon, too raw and too much, with Sanchez boxing beyond his years, cruising and counter punching and dominating the fight, finishing with an explosive combination in the fourteenth round which forced the referee to stop the fight.

Salvador Sanchez went on to become a dominating force in the featherweight division. On 12 August 1982, Sanchez was tragically killed in a car crash. He was twenty-three years old.

Danny Lopez retired in 1980 to then come back twelve years later to be stopped in two rounds. After a career of forty-eight contests, fighting in tough hard fights, with many being hellish, and taxing fights. The sparring wars in the gyms, and the punishment he absorbed, it was time.

A husband, a proud family man and a father to three boys, it was time for a new chapter in his life.

Danny 'Little Red' Lopez was a pugilistic hero to a generation, a throwback fighter who fought and gave a piece of himself every time he entered the ring to become the Featherweight champion of the world. Resilience, will, guts and heart. He was a warrior, and he was a native son from a time and place long gone but never forgotten.

CAREER TOTALS

Lopez retired with a fight record of 42 wins (39 KOs), 15 losses (6 KOs) and no draws.

I FOUGHT HARD. I TRIED MY BEST TO WIN. I FOUGHT IN A LOT OF TOUGH FIGHTS TO BECOME THE CHAMPION OF THE WORLD.

DANNY LOPEZ

What time did you get up in the morning?

6:00 am.

Did you do your roadwork in the morning?

Yes.

Did you stretch your body?

Yes. Full body stretching.

How far did you run?

I ran 6 miles.

What did you do after your run?

I would do 200 sit ups. My young boys would sit on my feet. Great memories.

What did you eat for breakfast?

I would eat raw eggs, orange juice water, eggs, and honey on toast.

What did you do after eating?

I would go for a nap. Rest up.

How many days did you train in the gym?

7 days in the gym.

What was your favourite exercise in the gym?

Sparring. It all had to be done but I liked sparring.

What time did you go to the gym?

I would train around 2:00 pm.

What time did you finish in the gym?

I trained for 2 hours every day.

What did you eat for dinner?

I liked steak. I had pasta, broccoli, and garlic. Orange juice and water.

Did you have a hobby or what do you do for fun?

I loved riding my Kawasaki dirt bike. I played golf, but mostly I loved spending time with my family. We would go to the mountains, fishing and camping.

Did you ever have a job?

I made pizza to get some money. I won the world title at 24. Things changed a bit after that. Later on, I worked as a labourer in construction.

What time did you go to sleep?

9:00 pm.

- Stretching – full body – 20 minutes.
- Jump rope – 6 minutes.
- Shadow box – 3 rounds x 3 minutes. (1 minute break between each round)
- Speed bag – 3 rounds x 3 minutes.
- Get ready for sparring.
- Sparring – 5–6 rounds of sparring x 3-minute rounds. (1 minute break between each round) 2 or 3 sparring partners changing.
- Heavy Bag – 4–5 rounds x 3 minutes. (1 minute break between each round)
- Sit ups – 120 of.
- 7 days in the gym.

GENNADY GOLOVKIN

'Damage'

BIOGRAPHY

Gennady Golovkin was born in the coal mining city of Karaganda, Kazakhstan in 1982.

Golovkin grew up in a public housing block with his Mother and Father and his three brothers in Maikuduk. Their urban playground was a tough industrial area with as many as twenty-five underground mines operating around the clock. The cold and damp concrete and soot-stained derelict buildings housed children playing games behind broken doors, and it was also a place for them to go to escape the freezing temperatures of the winter's days and nights.

Every day, Golovkin's father would clock in and walk the walk to the cable lift that would take him and countless other miners into the depths of blackness below.

As Golovkin and his twin brother Maxim played football in the streets, and the fields, their mother would come home from work to their small apartment, and she would make a boiled beef broth called *Besbarmak* for their family's dinner.

It was 1989. After listening to their older brothers about the importance of being strong and being able to defend themselves, the twin brothers walked into a boxing facility. It had one ring, a few bags, a bench and some weights and rubber mats spread across the hard floor. From that day on, the two young boys would go on a journey together, training, learning, watching, fighting and eventually campaigning in the amateurs together.

Golovkin's two brothers left Karaganda to serve in the Soviet Army.

In December 1991, after years of social disintegration, and bitter oppression, the fatherland of the Soviet Union dissolved. One nation would become fifteen republics, each following each other as time passed. Some flourished and some couldn't Some were the haves and some were the have-nots, with millions of people's lives altered and damaged during that time and for many years to come.

It was now 2004. Tragic, tough hard years had passed and there had been many changes in their lives.

Golovkin had qualified to represent Kazakhstan in the summer Olympic Games in Athens, winning a silver medal. With an impressive, decorated amateur record of 350 fights with only 5 losses, the twenty-two-year-old Golovkin was at a crossroads in his life.

Golovkin took a break from boxing to then make the difficult decision to leave his family and his homeland and move to Germany to pursue his dream of becoming a world champion.

Golovkin made his professional debut in 2006 and after dismantling his first eighteen opponents, he knew his future was in America. As a result of his varied cultural and professional background, Golovkin would become fluent in four languages - German, English, Russian and his native Kazakhstan.

In 2009, I remember getting a call from Anthony Mundine's promoter in Sydney. Mundine had recently beaten Daniel Geale in Australia, and he was now the IBO middleweight champion of the world. He asked me if I had heard of a guy from Germany called Golovkin? I told him I had and that I followed him in the amateurs and that he was a decorated Olympian. I also told him he was from Kazakhstan, not Germany. Mundine's promoter said, "Kazak where? ... Anyway, it doesn't matter to us. We have been offered to fight this guy in Germany, but we told them the fight has to be here in Australia".

I let him finish and said, "If you are asking me if you should take this fight, my view is you should stay well clear of this guy. He would break Anthony in half, inside two rounds."

He replied, "That's bullshit!", and hung up.

After destroying Mikhail Makarov in two rounds in November 2009, Golovkin packed his bag and made the trip to the west coast of America, to meet the experienced boxing trainer, Abel Sanchez. It was a meeting that would change his life.

Sanchez had a training facility in an idyllic lakeside town in the mountains of Southern California. Sitting at around six-thousand seven-hundred feet above sea level with it's long winding steep hills, 'Big Bear' was the perfect place to train at altitude, to run and recover in a serene environment, and for Golovkin, it was a place that felt like home.

It was now 2010. The twenty-eight-year-old Golovkin had made personal sacrifices for little gain in an unforgiving sport of broken promises, but his dream was still there.

After overwhelming Milton Núñez and knocking him out in fifty-eight seconds in Panama, he went back to Kazakhstan to stop the Colombian puncher, Nilson Julio Tapia with a vicious body punch in the third round to then beat the experienced and tough southpaw, Kassim Ouma in Panama City.

Golovkin was stepping up to face the Ugandan fighter but after a fast-paced torrid battle early on, Ouma faded, and Golovkin broke him down with a frenzied display of pressure and a controlled attack to his body, delivering sickening rips to his liver to then snap his head back with uppercuts, to finish him off in the tenth round of a brutal fight. The damage was done. Kassim Ouma fought on for another eleven years, but he was never the same.

Golovkin's travelling show continued as he went back to Germany to fight the 6'1 Philadelphian, Lajuan Simon for the vacant IBO middleweight world title, knocking him out with a big left hook in the first round. His first defence was against the Japanese champion, Makoto Fuchigami in Ukraine. Golovkin battered the brave southpaw into submission, putting him down in the second and third round, forcing the referee to step in.

It was now September 2012 and Golovkin's next opponent was the former two-time European champion, Grzegorz Proksa. The Polish southpaw was tough, and he had only lost once in twenty-nine fights. This was a big fight for Golovkin as it was his American TV debut.

In the fight, Golovkin hit Proksa with a piston like jab and hard thudding punches that broke him down as he cut the ring off, leaving him with little time to breathe. The proud and courageous Proksa succumbed to the savagery of the champion at 1:11 of the fifth round and he was never the same fighter after that night at the Turning Stone Casino.

Golovkin returned to New York to face the Philadelphia fighter, known as 'King' Gabriel Rosado. Golovkin was the King of Pain that night, as he dismantled and banged up Rosado using his jab, dominating the fight, and leaving him in survival mode as he struggled with the incoming onslaught to his badly cut left eye and nose. With blood everywhere, the fight was stopped in the seventh round.

Golovkin then packed his bags to face the unbeaten (25-win) Japanese puncher, Nobuhiro Ishida in Monaco. Golovkin knocked him out in the third round.

Next up was the talented and durable fighter from Birmingham, England, Matthew Macklin. Golovkin stalked and pressured Macklin, leaving him visibly shaken as he took some heavy thudding punches. Macklin fired back bravely but he was caught with a perfect left rip to the body that sent him down in agony to the canvas, where he stayed for some time after he was counted out in the third round.

After three fights in five months, Golovkin had a vacation then went straight back to Big Bear to train for the New York puncher, Curtis Stevens. Known as 'The Cerebral Assassin' he was short but powerful and he was street tough.

In the fight, Golovkin took some to give some but as the rounds went on, Stevens was retreating to the ropes and Golovkin chopped him down, leaving him, and his primal instinct and all he ever knew to suddenly be trapped inside a body that couldn't respond or adapt to the savagery of Golovkin in the eighth round.

It was now February 2014. Golovkin was back in Monaco to face the puncher from Accra, Ghana, Adama Osumanu.

Known as 'Machine Gun' Adamu had won twenty-two fights with sixteen knockouts. In the fight, Golovkin was machine like, using his superb jab, and going to the body and connecting with big uppercuts that hurt Adamu, sending him down with a jab to then hammer him until the referee had seen enough in the seventh round.

A few months later, Golovkin took on the challenge from the Australian boxer, and former world champion, Daniel Geale in New York in his thirtieth fight. At stake was the WBA and IBO championship belts. In the fight, Geale was there to fight, as he tried to push Golovkin backwards, with the game plan of trying to unsettle him and outbox him. Geale was knocked down in the second round to then be caught by a hard right hand as he was trying to throw one of his own. He was knocked down but rose up on unsteady legs and the referee stopped the fight in the third round. Three months later, he battered the experienced sixty-six-fight, Mexican, Marco Antonio Rubio in two rounds.

Martin Murray had fought his way into contention for a crack at Golovkin in 2015. With a tremendous record of thirty-one fights with his only loss to Sergio Martinez, Murray was the number one contender for a reason. He was a proud, durable fighter who always came to fight. In the fight, Murray fought with heart, throwing everything he had while taking heavy fire from Golovkin, and going down early in the fight. The spirited Murray recovered and kept coming forward, but he didn't have the power to trouble Golovkin, but he connected with a variety of punch combinations that unsettled the champion from Kazakhstan. In the end, Golovkin was unyielding, chipping away to Murray's body with his relentless pressure and power punching, hurting him in the tenth round to force the stoppage in the eleventh round.

Golovkin would fight two more fights in that year. He overwhelmed the slick and awkward southpaw, Willie Monroe Jnr. in six rounds, to then out punch and dismantle the Canadian David Lemieux in a show of strength, power and skill in a unification match in New York.

After a demolishing the unbeaten Dominic Wade in two rounds, Golovkin travelled to London to face the unbeaten 36-0 Sheffield fighter, Kell Brook. The Englishman was the undisputed welterweight champion of the world, but he decided to move up two weight divisions to challenge Golovkin. Brook was a naturally big welterweight, so the transition seemed natural to him.

In the fight, Brook used his fast hands to catch Golovkin with upper cuts and straight right hands, but the champion was unfazed. Golovkin stalked Brook, hurting him in the first round to go on to systematically break him down with solid jabs and left hooks to his head. With Brook's right eye starting to swell, Golovkin threw laser accurate hooks that sent Brook backwards as he poured on the pain. Golovkin's ram rod jab was snapping Brook's head back and he was breaking the Sheffield champion down. In the end, the destructive power and the damage was too much. Brook's right eye socket was broken, and the towel was thrown into the ring in the fifth round.

It was now early 2017. Golovkin was the unified middleweight champion.

Next up was the 'Miracle Man' Daniel Jacobs. With one loss in thirty-three fights, Jacobs was a big strong middleweight who could box and punch and had speed of both foot and hand. Known for having a huge heart, he was also a survivor of a rare bone cancer. Jacobs was going into the fight with confidence, pride and passion.

In the fight, with nothing to lose and everything to gain, Jacobs fought tremendously well, taking the fight to the smaller Golovkin. After a closely fought fight, with Jacobs going down in the fourth round, and being staggered in the championship rounds, the fight went to the judges' scorecards. The scores were 115–112 twice and 114–113. The knockdown and the accuracy of the power punches inside were the difference in the fight.

It was a great fight, but all the talk was about the Mexican superstar, Saul 'Canelo' Alvarez.

The fight was two years in the making as the two champions followed their own paths. The fight was signed for September in Las Vegas.

Alvarez had been fighting for twelve years with his only loss to Floyd Mayweather at junior middleweight in 2013.

In the fight, Golovkin fought smarter, better and he pressured Alvarez, making him retreat to the ropes to then keep him in check with his jab, and right hand. Golovkin gave Alvarez little chance to breathe and by the sixth round, the Mexican was gassing out as he was cradled on the ropes.

Alvarez came back in the ninth round with a big uppercut that hurt Golovkin to then connect with a hard right hand that bounced off his head. There were a couple of close rounds but when I sat at ringside, I had Golovkin winning comfortably, and Alvarez needing a spectacular knockout in the championship rounds to win, but he never came close. Golovkin chased and rallied hard until the final bell, and to the judges' scorecards. It was a superb performance from Golovkin. I had him winning the fight, seven rounds to Alvarez's five.

The scores were, 115-113, 114-114 to Golovkin, from two of the judges at ringside. The other judge scored the fight to Alvarez, with a staggering 118-110 score. That judge had Alvarez winning ten rounds, and she gave the unified middleweight champion of the world two rounds. It was a disgrace and an embarrassment to the sport of boxing, and it was incompetence at the highest level on the world's stage of sports.

The rematch was signed for May 2018 in Las Vegas on the Cinco De Mayo Mexican holiday weekend. Golovkin trained quietly but harder than ever. With only two months to go, it was announced that the fight was off due to Alvarez failing a mandatory drug test. The Mexican was banned from boxing for six months.

Golovkin fought on and with a change of city and venue, a new opponent had to be found.

Vanes Martirosyan was a tough, Armenian fighter who had three losses in forty fights. He had faced Demetrius Andrade, Jermell Charlo and Erislandy Lara at junior middleweight in recent years. Golovkin destroyed him in two rounds. Martirosyan never fought again.

It was then announced that Golovkin would face Alvarez in September in Las Vegas on the Mexican holiday weekend of Independence Day.

In the fight, Alvarez targeted the body of Golovkin, ripping fast hard punches in, to follow up with strong jabs to win the early rounds. Golovkin came back strong from round seven on, using his jab, and pressure and his undeniable will to win. Alvarez won the final round in a gruelling war of attrition. With both warriors cut and black and blue, it was up to the judges once more. The judges scored 115-113, 115-113, and 114-114. It was a closely fought fight, but Alvarez won by a majority decision. It was a fantastic fight that could have gone either way.

Golovkin took a well-deserved break to then return in June 2019 to fight the unbeaten (19-win), Steve Rolls, in a catch weight fight at 163Lbs. Golovkin wreaked havoc on the Canadian boxer, leaving him down and out in the fourth round in New York.

Golovkin returned four months later to fight the hard as nails, Ukrainian, Sergiy Derevyanchenko in New York. At stake was the vacant IBO and IBF middleweight championship belts. The Ukrainian fighter had lost to Daniel Jacobs by a split decision in 2018.

In the fight, the thirty-seven-year-old Golovkin knocked Derevyanchenko down in the first round, but he rose to his feet and came back and fought with a brave heart and a will to win, taking the fight to Golovkin, as he went to the body of the man known as GGG. Golovkin and Derevyanchenko went into battle for twelve hard rounds but when the war was over, Golovkin's hand was raised, winning on points at Madison Square Garden in his forty second contest.

Golovkin came back, fourteen months later and hammered the former two-time European champion, Kamil Szeremeta over seven rounds to then break down and stop the Japanese Olympic Gold medallist, Ryota Murata in the ninth round in Japan in April 2022.

Golovkin, now forty years old, could have retired, but he fought in a trilogy fight with Saul Alvarez. The historic fight was for the unified super middleweight championship of the world. Alvarez won by a unanimous points decision in Las Vegas.

Gennady Golovkin retired in 2022.

After fighting in forty-five fights, with thirty-seven knockouts, and boxing for close to thirty years, it was time to go.

Golovkin was a complete fighting machine. A superb boxer. A master of distance, space and timing. An accurate puncher, with an unshakable granite chin, he was an immovable force in the middleweight division.

He achieved greatness as the unified champion of the world.

The damage was done.

CAREER TOTALS

Golovkin walked away from boxing with a fight record of 42 wins (37 KOs), 2 losses and 1 draw.

What time do you get up in the morning?

5:00 am.

Do you do your roadwork in the morning?

Yes. I stretch and warm my body and run at 54 5:00 am.

Do you stretch your body?

Yes. Stretch all day.

How far do you run?

4 miles every day.

What do you do after your run?

I go to gym and do stretching and I do sit up exercises.

What do you eat for breakfast?

Porridge or oatmeal. Eggs, berry smoothies.

What do you do after eating?

I rest, relax.

How many days do you train in the gym?

6 days.

What is your favourite exercise in the gym?

Everything has to be done. I like the water bag (hydra bag).

Do you eat lunch?

Yes. Light some chicken grilled. Salad and some small rice. Fresh fruit smoothie.

What time do you go to the gym?

3:00 pm. I love training. I am lucky.

What time do you finish in the gym?

Around 5:00 pm.

What do you eat for dinner?

I like braised or grilled steak. I eat fish, shrimp. We eat Mexican food. Healthy clean. Vegetables garlic, salads.

Do you have a hobby or what do you like to do for fun?

Listen to music. Watch TV. I read. Go for walk. I like nice things. Clothes fashion.
I like sports and soccer.

Did you ever have a job?

Always boxer.

What time do you go to sleep?

9:30 pm.

NON-SPARRING DAYS

- Stretching – 15 minutes.
- Skipping – 10 minutes non-stop.
- Shadow box – 2 x 3-minute rounds.
- Focus mitts and punch shield – 4 x 3-minute rounds.
- Heavy bag – 4 rounds x 3 minutes.
- Double end bag – 2 x 3-minute rounds.
- Hydro (water filled) bag – 2 x 3-minute rounds.
- Sit ups routine – 1200 total.

ROADWORK AND RUNNING

- Golovkin runs at an altitude of more than 7000 ft (2100 meters) above sea level.
- The air is thinner at that altitude, and it takes athletes around ten days to acclimate.

Monday, Wednesday and Friday

- Stretching, warm up, shadow box.
- Roadwork – 4 miles total.
- After running, Golovkin does stretching and 1200 of sit up exercises.
- Sit ups sitting on a bench.
- Sit up twists.
- Sit up twists holding a 35-pound weight plate.
- Alternating Side crunches.
- Leg raises.

Tuesday and Thursday

- Stretching, warm up, shadow box.
- Golovkin does interval sprints.
- Short explosive sprints.
- Longer explosive sprints.
- Short explosive sprints.
- Adding up to around 3.5 miles total.
- Go to gym straight after and do 15 minutes of stretching and then 1200 sit ups (same as Mon, Wednesday and Friday)
- Saturday – Golovkin runs up and down the hills of Big Bear for 9 miles.
- Stretching and sit ups x 1500 of.
- Sunday off. Rest relax recover.
- Active recovery ongoing is massage, steam room, sauna, swimming and ice bath.

SPARRING DAYS

- Stretching – 15 minutes. Arms, back, legs. Full body.
- Skipping – 10 minutes non-stop.
- Shadow box in the ring – 2 x 3-minute rounds.
- Focus Mitts and Punch shield – 4 x 3-minute rounds.
- Heavy Bag – 3 x 3-minute rounds.
- Sparring begins – 4 sparring partners on rotation. Hard and intense sparring.
- Sparring – 8–10 rounds x 3 minutes.
- Resistance bands.
- Double end bag – 2 x 3-minute rounds.
- Hydro (water filled) Bag – working on single power left and right hooks or overhand hooks.
- Sit ups – 1000 of.
- Sit ups.
- Sit up twists, holding a 35-pound weight plate.
- Side crunches alternating.
- Leg raises.

STRENGTH TRAINING

- Stretching – full body. Move around. – 15 minutes.
- Skipping in the ring – 10 minutes.

- Sit ups – 1200 total.
- Sit ups.
- Side crunches alternating.
- Sit ups with 35-pound weight plate.
- Sit ups alternating twists.
- Leg raises.
- Into the ring – holding a 2 lb hand weight. Non-stop circuit.
- Light weight dumbbell punching out straight, alternating at shoulder level. – 3 minutes non-stop.
- Light weight punching out alternating at shoulder level in a hooking motion for 3 minutes non-stop. (1 minute rest between each 3 minutes of work)
- Shadow boxing and moving around with light dumbbells for 3 minutes non-stop x 3.
- Light dumbbells – flies up and down for 1 minute.
- Lightweight dumbbells flies in and outwards at chest level for 1 minute.
- Dumbbells alternating straight up above your head and down to shoulder level and up. 1 minute.
- Dumbbells alternating with arms punching straight out at chest level for 1 minute.
- Dumbbells out straight out to the sides and hold and while arms straight out, begin to make controlled circling motions without letting your arms drop down to your sides. 1 minute.
- Same exercise but do circling motion in reverse for 1 minute.
- Dumbbells with arms completely straight out in front of you at shoulder level. Begin alternating your arms up and down without letting your arms drop down, keeping your arms straight for 1 minute.

Note: the above is changed up by using a short light barbell. Similar exercises in circuit.

- Neck exercises – lie down on your stomach. Arms behind your back. Put your forehead on a cushion or a thick pad or towel. Focus on lifting your mid-section off the floor. There will be strain on your head and neck and your feet.
- Head harness on – the harness has a weight hanging from it. As the weight plate hangs down, lift your head up and down and side to side alternating. 30 of x 3 repetitions.
- Push ups.
- Jumps up and down with 12lb medicine ball.
- Squat jumps with 12lb medicine ball.
- Pushing 12lb medicine ball as a shoulder press.
- Pull ups.
- Resistance training band.
- Sit ups routine as noted x 1200 of total.

Note: Golovkin changes his circuit training up as camp progresses.

He also incorporates, kettle bell rolls. He has his forearm flat on the mat. The kettle bell is on its side. Golovkin grabs the handle and rolls it over, right to left then alternating arm rolling kettle bell from left to right.

Active Recovery is sauna, steam room, ice bath and swimming.

NATE CAMPBELL

'Born to Fight'

BIOGRAPHY

Two young boys skipped and ran through the sunburned grass that took them into the waste ground where their dilapidated neighbourhood had been thrown up. It was their crib, and it was all they had. They would leave every day to go and collect water for their kin and when they returned, if they were lucky, they would eat. They would be messing around playing, and laughing until they saw a junkie, wasted on crack cocaine, slumped over in a doorway or hearing the noise of a woman wailing a desperate cry for help from behind a broken window in a building full of broken people. Every day, the junkies, the dealers, the pimps and the 'hoes' would take their nine-year-old minds into a world of violence and chaos.

They ran like rabbits until they reached the corner then they would look at each other and laugh again. It was 1981.

Nate Campbell was born in the port city of Jacksonville, Florida in 1972. He grew up in the dope-stricken inner-city housing projects with his mother, father and siblings, and thousands of African American families who were all living and trying to survive the epidemic that was crack cocaine. Unemployment, recession, hopelessness and Afro-Americans killing other Afro-Americans with a bullet, or white lines.

If life wasn't hard enough, when Campbell was five years old, his mother, a heroin addict, was sent to prison, leaving him to be placed into the foster care system. A few years later, on Campbell's tenth birthday, his father passed away from an ongoing illness.

In a neighbourhood of violence, of hungry children, where saints became sinners while looking for their next fix, Campbell fought through the pain. He wiped his tears and gritted his teeth and although the scars and bitter memories would always be there, he kept moving forward. Some struggled, some hustled, some fought, some fell through the cracks, and most of them watched their dreams fly away like birds in the sky.

Campbell was precocious, an artful dodger, a dark horse.

But most of all he was a fighter.

He took up boxing in 1997, campaigning in the amateurs to then turn professional in February 2000 at the age of twenty-eight.

After racking up a 23-win-, no-defeat-record in only two years, Campbell was matched to face the 29-win-, 1-loss-Cuban southpaw, Joel Casamayor in Temecula, California. Casamayor was a tough, experienced cagey boxer who had three hundred and ninety-three amateur fights, losing only thirty. He won the gold medal in the 1992 Olympic games in Barcelona to then defect to the United States in 1996. His only professional loss was to the big punching Brazilian, Acelino Freitas in a world title unification fight at super featherweight in 2002.

Going into the fight, Campbell was a big underdog while Casamayor's mind was narrowed with thoughts of a Freitas rematch. In the fight, Campbell jabbed, feinted and countered the Cuban slickster to win the first three rounds. Casamayor won the middle rounds with Campbell rallying back with uppercuts and going to the body of the bigger man. With both fighters cut from head clashes, the fight went the full ten rounds. The judges' scorecards were 97–93, 99–92, and 96–94, with Casamayor winning by a unanimous decision. Campbell did enough to win the fight, and he should have had his hand raised that night in Temecula. It was a bitter loss, but Campbell kept going. Three months later, he fought Edelmiro Martinez in Atlantic City, fighting ten rounds to get a draw. After waiting seven months for an opponent, Campbell took his frustrations out on Daniel Attah, knocking him down three times over the twelve rounds to start 2004 off with a tremendous victory. Next up was the aggressive Australian, Robbie Peden.

In the fight, Peden threw combinations while Peden used his jab to follow up with his power right hand. It was a close fight until the fifth round. Campbell had been targeting the body of Peden in the previous rounds, and he was breaking him down. Campbell hit Peden with a sickening body shot that bent the brave Australian fighter over in agony, but he recovered and continued to box. It seemed like it was only a matter of time for Peden to fold, but unbelievably Campbell dropped his two hands in the middle of the ring and Peden threw a big left hook that landed, which sent Campbell down and out in his twenty seventh fight.

Campbell returned to the gym and trained angry, to then face Edelmiro Martinez in a rematch. In the fight, Campbell came out very fast and battered 'The Tiger' to the body in a strong display of controlled aggression, speed and power. Edelmiro went down three times in round two after a heavy onslaught of pressure punching. Campbell was deducted one point for a low blow and Edelmiro was deducted two points for excessive low blows, to finally be disqualified in the fourth round.

Edelmiro Martinez never fought again.

It was then announced that Campbell would be going down under to fight Robbie 'Bomber' Peden again, but this time in Melbourne. At stake was the vacant super featherweight world title. Going into the fight, Peden trained hard, sparring Shane Mosley in preparation for the biggest fight of his life. In the fight, Campbell was fighting desperate as he was cut badly over his right eye. Peden fought with desire and he out fought Campbell, opening up his left eye with his punches and also head clashes on the inside. With Campbell cut and bloodied, Peden poured on the pressure and the referee stepped in to stop the fight in the eighth round.

Peden went on to face the Mexican legendary fighter, Marco Antonio Barrera in a unification fight later that year and he was outboxed over twelve rounds in Las Vegas.

Campbell fought on, winning and losing to close out 2005 with a tremendous 'underdog' knockout win over the highly touted boxer from Kyrgyzstan, Almazbek Raiymkulov, in St Petersburg, Tampa. The man known as 'Kid Diamond' was undefeated as a professional and he had recently fought and roughed up Casamayor to then be duped in a draw in New York. Campbell out classed and stopped the rough diamond in the tenth round.

Campbell challenged the South African IBO lightweight champion of the world, Isaac Hlatshwayo in April 2006, but lost on a split decision in a tough fight. From there he won three fights in a row which put him in line to challenge the undefeated (33-win) lightweight champion of the world, Juan 'Baby Bull' Diaz for the WBC, WBO and IBF belts. The unification fight was staged in Mexico in the bull fighting ring of 'The Plaza De Toros'.

Diaz was a twenty-four-year-old, strong, aggressive pressure fighter and once again, Campbell was going into the fight as a huge underdog.

Going into the fight, after a tremendous training camp, Campbell went to his church to visit his longtime Pastor Willie Frank Robinson but when he got there, he was told that he was in hospital. Campbell went to him as he lay very sick in his bed, and they talked about their relationship through the years and the fight with Diaz. As Campbell was leaving, his friend and father figure Pastor said to him, "Go and win the fight. I'll be with you." Campbell left the quiet room and cried alone.

As Campbell walked through the Mexican crowd in Cancun, the light shone down on him as in his mind, the Pastor was now in the arms of the angels and watching down on him.

In the fight, Campbell came out hard and fast, going to the champions body and hitting him with uppercuts and right hands. Diaz, known for his volume punching couldn't breathe as the challenger poured on the pressure. In round six, Campbell was deducted one point for a head butt that was in fact, a punch. Campbell remained focused and continued to work the body of Diaz. With blood streaming down the champions face, Campbell's will to win, and relentless pressure was the difference in a great fight that went the championship distance. It was in the hands of the judges but there could only be one winner. Nate Campbell, at age thirty-six, was the unified lightweight champion of the world. After his hand was raised up in victory, he sounded the words, "Pastor, you can go home." It was a tremendous, emotional and inspirational moment as he fought and won the fight of his life.

Now the number one lightweight in the world, Campbell was to face Joan Guzman in his first defence, but Guzman failed to make the weight, and the fight was called off.

It was now February 2009. Eleven months had passed. Campbell was matched to fight Ali Funeka in Sunrise, Florida but going into the fight, the champion failed to make the weight and in turn, he was stripped of his world titles. The fight went ahead, and Campbell won on points.

He moved up to the super lightweight division to challenge Timothy Bradley but was outboxed before taking a bad cut to his fragile left eye from an accidental head butt and the fight was stopped and ruled as a no contest.

Campbell then went on to lose to Walter Estrada and Danny Garcia on points. Inactivity in the ring and Father Time was a fight he couldn't win. He was now thirty-nine years old, yet he still fought on, fighting in Russia, Dominican Republic, England and Poland until 2014. He fought and won in his fiftieth fight in Florida, and he retired thereafter and enjoyed his life with his family.

Campbell briefly returned to the ring in 2024 as a welterweight.

Nate Campbell defied the odds many times in his life. He fought the battle inside. Every fight was a test of his soul, to find out what he had inside, and to see how far he could reach down to then rise up stronger. From being the underdog to being left behind to becoming the unified champion of the world.

He was 'The Galaxxy Warrior' and he was born to fight.

CAREER TOTALS

Campbell retired from the sport of boxing with a fight record of 38 wins (26 KOs), 11 losses (4 KOs) and 1 draw.

NATE CAMPBELL – A DAY IN THE LIFE

What time did you get up in the morning?

Around 7:00 am.

Did you run in the morning?

No, I ran at 11:30 pm at night.

How far did you run?

I ran 4–6 miles every night.

Did you stretch before you run?

No.

What did you do after your roadwork?

I showered and then I lay down to sleep.

What did you eat for breakfast?

I had spinach and mushrooms and some eggs. Orange juice and water.

What did you do after eating?

I would get myself ready for the gym.

What time did you train in the gym?

I would go to the gym at 9:00 am and train until 11:00 am.

How many days in the gym?

6 days.

What was your favourite exercise in the gym?

Everything had to be done, but I liked sparring.

What did you eat for dinner?

It depended on the training camp, but I had grilled chicken, greens, asparagus, juice and water.

What did you do for fun or a hobby?

I enjoyed hanging out with the guys in the gym. Randall Bailey, and Charles Whittaker. We were like the rat pack. Laughing and joking. I liked reading and watching movies. When I was a kid, we didn't have a TV or a radio, so I used to read. I like basketball and I love comedies.

Did you ever have a job?

Yes. I worked as a salesman. I worked filling shelves at night.

What time did you go to sleep?

Around 1:00am. After I run, I had to decompress.

NON-SPARRING DAYS

- Wrap hands.
- Jump rope – 3–4 rounds.
- Shadow box – 4 x 4-minute rounds 30-second break in between rounds.
- Glove up.
- Focus mitts – 6 x 4-minute rounds – 30-second breaks between each 4-minutes.
- Heavy bag – 4 x 4-minute rounds.
- 30-second breaks between each round.
- Uppercut bag – 4 x 4-minute rounds 30-second breaks between each 4-minutes.
- Double end bag – 4 x 4-minute rounds 30-second break between each round.
- Speed bag – 4 x 4-minute rounds with a 30-second break between each round.
- Stomach exercises:
- Rack knees up knees up from floor to chest and repeat. 4 x 4-minute durations. 30-second break between each 4-minutes.
- Sit ups x 200 of.
- Pull ups x 4 sets of 10 repetitions.
- Cool-down – moving around.

SPARRING DAYS

- Wrap hands.
- Shadow box – 4 x 4-minute rounds.
- 30-second break.
- Glove up.
- Sparring – 9 x 4-minute rounds with 30-second breaks in between each round.
- We used 3 sparring partners on rotation.
- Heavy bag – 3 x 4-minute rounds.
- 30-second breaks in between rounds.
- Uppercut hook bag – 3 x 4-minute rounds with a 30-second break in between each 4-minutes of work.
- Speed bag – 3 x 4-minute rounds.
- 30-second break in between rounds.
- Double end bag – 3 x 4-minute rounds with a 30-second break between rounds.
- Stomach exercises:
- Rack Knees up from floor to chest x 4-minutes x 4.
- Sit ups – 200 of.
- Pull ups 4 x 10 of.
- Cool down – moving around.

ABOUT THE AUTHOR

GARY TODD

Gary Todd was born and raised out of tough times in Dundee, Scotland.

He has been involved in all aspects of the sport of boxing as a coach and mentor and as a cut man and a boxing writer and a big fight pundit for decades.

He has walked the walk and talked the talk with regard to training with and interviewing the greatest boxers and legendary fighters from around the world. His passion has always been for the fighters and the young boxers and what they did in the gym. He is an ambassador for the sport of boxing and he has always represented the people away from the bright lights, who work hard in the shadows.

He is an acclaimed international best selling author with his books and his boxing analysis is sought after by sky sports and ESPN. He writes from experience and he writes from his heart.

GARY TODD – A DAY IN THE LIFE

What time do you get up in the morning?

5:45 am. I'm up and out. I go to work.

What do you have for breakfast?

I eat tuna and onion mixed. I like mixed berries, and I'll have a banana. I'll drink healthy fresh juices. I don't eat bread from Monday to Friday. Saturday and Sunday, I'll treat myself to crispy bacon.

What time do you go to the gym?

I finish work around 5:00 pm and I go straight to the gym or the pool.

What time do you finish training?

I train hard, non-stop for an hour and a half. It's about training smart. You don't need to spend hours in the gym. It's *how* you train. It's about showing up.

What is your favourite exercise in the gym?

I've always enjoyed sparring, but I like hitting the double end bag. I love skipping. It all has to be done.

How many days do you train?

I do something most days. Boxing training and alternating with swimming and steam room.

What do you do after training?

I go home. My dog takes me for a walk! I have dinner and relax.

What do you eat for dinner?

I eat light lunch. Sushi and fruit. For dinner, I like chicken, fish, steak, salads. Pasta once a week. I like my wife's cooking. Homemade mushroom soup and cauliflower soup. I drink fizzy water. Water or juices and Coke Zero.

Do you have any hobbies or what do you do for fun?

World boxing (both amateur and professional) has always been a passion for me. I enjoy writing about boxing. I enjoy painting boxing. I love music and I love my dog. I also enjoy swimming in the ocean.

What job do you do?

I am a construction boss.

What time do you go to sleep?

I go to bed around 8:45 pm. I like to get 8 hours sleep.

Monday Wednesday Friday

- Stretching 15 minutes.
- Shadow Box 6 minutes non-stop.
- Light dumbbells – 2.5 kg.
- Punch out drills – shoulder height 100 x of.
- Arm Curls alternating 100 x of.
- Shoulder flies with 2.5 kg dumbbells 100 x of.
- Floor to Ceiling 10 minutes non-stop OR Speed Bag 3 rounds x 3 minutes with a 1-minute break.
- 6 kg medicine ball front raise while standing (focus on stomach as you raise ball up above your head and then control and focus while lowering. 50 x of.
- Stationary Bike 30 minutes (10 kilometres) medium strain.
- Walk around.
- Lift heavy stone. 10 x lift. [100 kg – 220 pounds]
- Finish off Juggling balls 5 minutes.
- Take my dog for a walk 25 minutes.

Tuesday, Thursday and Saturday – Swimming and Steam Room

- Steam room – 25 minutes.
- Drink water – go into the pool.
- Swimming – walk up and down 25-metre pool.
- Swim underwater for 25 metres x 4 laps.
- Swim 25 metres x 4 laps.
- Drink water – back into steam room.
- Steam room – 20 minutes. Drink water.
- Return to the pool –
- Walk 25 metres of pool x 2.
- Swim under water – 25 metre pool x 3 laps.
- Swim 25 metre x 3 laps.
- Drink water.
- Back into the Steam Room – 15 minutes. Drink water.
- Return to pool.
- Walk 25 metre x 1 lap.
- Swim under water x 2 laps of pool.
- Swim 2 laps of 25 metre pool.
- Drink water.
- Back into Steam Room – 10 minutes.
- Drink water.
- Return to the pool – walk up and down the pool. Relax.
- Cool down – Relax and breathe. Drink water.

- Try to swim in the ocean as much as possible, if you have an ocean nearby, or a river, if it's safe. The cold water is good for your body. It's a great feeling. It makes you feel alive.
- Eat a balanced diet – good food, salads, vegetables, and protein. Reduce your intake of carbohydrates such as bread and pasta but don't go crazy by completely stopping. You've got to live!
- Drink water.
- Live a happy life and work hard but remember to treat yourself at the weekends and holidays.
- Live and love life.

AFTERWORD

I hope you enjoyed reading my book and I hope it gave you an insight into their life as a boxer and what they endured to be great.

Each of them went on a journey and they all walked on a long, hard road that only they could walk.

Discipline, hard work, grit, determination and a belief deep inside them is what made them champions.

We can't all be champions of the world, but we can be the best version of ourselves every day and we can all reach for the stars and make our own dreams and goals become a reality if we keep going strong and we are willing to walk the long road ahead.

Thank you to Everlast for all they do in the sport of boxing.

PROFESSIONAL DIVISION WEIGHTS

Division Name	MEN Weight	WOMEN Weight
Strawweight	up to **105 lbs** (47.7 kg)	up to 102 lbs (46.3 kg)
Mini-Flyweight/		up to 105 lbs (47.7 kg)
Junior Flyweight	105-**108 lbs** (49.1 kg)	105-108 lbs(49.1 kg)
Flyweight	108-**112 lbs** (50 kg)	108-112 lbs (50 kg)
Super Flyweight/ Junior Bantamweight	112-**115 lbs** (52.3 kg)	112-115 lbs (52.3 kg)
Bantamweight	115-**118 lbs** (53.6 kg)	115-118 lbs (53.6 kg)
Super Bantamweight/ Junior Featherweight	118-**122 lbs** (55.5 kg)	118-122 lbs (55.5 kg)
Featherweight	122-**126 lbs** (57.3 kg)	122-126 lbs (57.3 kg)
Super Featherweight/ Junior Lightweight	126-**130 lbs** (59.1 kg)	126-130 lbs (59.1 kg)
Lightweight	130-**135 lbs** (61.4 kg)	130-135 lbs (61.4 kg)
Super Lightweight/ Junior Welterweight	135-**140 lbs** (63.6 kg)	135-140 lbs (63.6 kg)
Welterweight	140-**147 lbs** (66.8 kg)	140-147 lbs (66.8 kg)
Super Welterweight/ Junior Middleweight	147 -**154 lbs** (70 kg)	147-154 lbs (70 kg)
Middleweight	154-**160 lbs** (72.7 kg)	154-160 lbs (72.7 kg)
Super Middleweight	160-**168 lbs** (76.4 kg)	160-168 lbs (76.4 kg)
Light Heavyweight	168-**175 lbs** (79 kg)	168-175 lbs (79 kg)
Cruiserweight	175-**200 lbs** (90 kg)	
Heavyweight	**over 200 lbs** (91.4 kg+)	over 175 lbs (79.5 kg+)

AMATEUR DIVISION WEIGHTS

Division Name	MEN Weight	WOMEN Weight
Pin weight		up to 101 lbs (46 kg)
Light Flyweight	up to **106 lbs** (48 kg)	101-106 lbs (48 kg)
Flyweight	106-**112 lbs** (51 kg)	106-11 0 lbs (50 kg)
Light Bantamweight/		110-114 lbs (52 kg)
Bantamweight	112-**119 lbs** (54 kg)	114-119 lbs (54 kg)
Featherweight	119-**125 lbs** (57 kg)	119-125 lbs (57 kg)
Lightweight	125-**132 lbs** (60 kg)	125-132 lbs (60 kg)
Light Welterweight	132-**141 lbs** (64 kg)	132-138 lbs (63 kg)
Welterweight	141-**152 lbs** (69 kg)	138-145 lbs (66 kg)
Light Middleweight/		145-154 lbs (70 kg)
Middleweight	165-**178 lbs** (75 kg)	154-165 lbs (75 kg)
Light Heavyweight	165-**178 lbs** (81 kg)	165-17 6 lbs (80 kg)
Heavyweight	178-**201 lbs** (91 kg)	17 6-189 lbs (86 kg)
Super Heavyweight	**201 lbs and up** (91 kg+)	189 lbs and up (86 kg+)

BOXER PICTURE CREDITS

Artwork of Gennady Golovkin, Marvelous Marvin Hagler, Tim Tszyu, Deontay Wilder, Azumah Nelson, Sergio Martinez, Danny Lopez, and Vito Antuofermo, designs by Gary Todd.

Artwork drawn by Georgia Delaportas. Used with permission.

Cassius Baloyi – Cassius' private collection.

Manuel Medina – © Mary Ann Lurie Owen. Used with permission.

Angel Manfredy – © Pat Orr. Used with permission.

Michael Olajide Jnr. – © lev radin | Shutterstock.

Lester Ellis – Lester's private collection. Used with permission.

Jesse James Leija – from his Facebook page.

Gary Jacobs – © Jim Diamond. Used with permission.

Vassiliy Jirov, Carlos Palomino, Yaqui Lopez, Gerry Cooney, Nate Campbell – Personal collection.

Mike Weaver – © Linda Platt. Used with permission.

George Kambosos Jnr. – © Dylan Allen. Used with permission.

Sakio Bika – Used with permission from Sakio.

Steve Collins –page 130 Collection of Gary Todd.
– page 139 © Mark Grasso, *The Boston Herald*. Used with permission.

Jai Opetaia – Jai's private collection. Used with permission.

Vic Toweel – Collection of Paul Toweel. Used with permission.

Gary Todd – © Dominic Spagnolo. Used with permission.

Every effort has been made to trace the copyright holders and obtain permission to reproduce this material. Please do get in touch with any enquiries or any information relating to this image or the rights holder.